CUPCAKE COOKBOOK

Step by Step Recipes of Chocolate Cupcake Desserts & Buttercream

(Delicious Cupcake Recipes for Any Event)

Ronald Collins

Published by Sharon Lohan

© Ronald Collins

All Rights Reserved

Cupcake Cookbook: Step by Step Recipes of Chocolate Cupcake Desserts & Buttercream (Delicious Cupcake Recipes for Any Event)

ISBN 978-1-7776245-6-9

All rights reserved. No part of this guide may be reproduced in any form without permission in writing from the publisher except in the case of brief quotations embodied in critical articles or reviews.

Legal & Disclaimer

The information contained in this book is not designed to replace or take the place of any form of medicine or professional medical advice. The information in this book has been provided for educational and entertainment purposes only.

The information contained in this book has been compiled from sources deemed reliable, and it is accurate to the best of the Author's knowledge; however, the Author cannot guarantee its accuracy and validity and cannot be held liable for any errors or omissions. Changes are periodically made to this book. You must consult your doctor or get professional medical advice before using any of the suggested remedies, techniques, or information in this book.

Table of contents

Part 1 1
Introduction 2
Cupcake Recipes 4
Sweetheart Cupcakes: 4
Vegan Cupcakes: 5
Meatloaf Cupcakes: 6
Frog Cupcakes: 7
Cupcake Graveyard: 8
Lasagna Cupcakes: 9
Bat Cupcakes 11
Chocolate Cupcakes: 12
Easy Black Bottom Cupcakes: 13
Brownie Cupcakes: 13
Zucchini Raspberry Cupcakes: 15
Spider Cupcakes: 15
Chocolate Fudge Cupcakes: 17
Molten Chocolate Cupcakes With Sugar Coated Raspberries: 18
Red Velvet Cupcakes: 19
Mini Cheesecakes: 20
Lemon Cupcakes: 21
Apple Banana Cupcakes: 23
Harvest Pumpkin Cupcakes: 23
Vanilla Cupcakes: 24
Peanut Butter Cupcakes: 26
Cupcake Princess Vanilla Cupcakes: 27

- Oreo Mini Philly Cheesecakes: 27
- Miniature Cheesecakes: 29
- Rainbow Cupcakes: 30
- Easy Chocolate Cupcakes: 31
- Bari's Banana Cupcakes: 32
- Cone Cupcakes: 33
- Salad Dressing Cupcakes: 33
- Super Easy Chocolate Cupcakes: 35
- Lemon Lime Cupcakes: 35
- Eastern Surprise Cupcakes: 37
- Banana Vanilla Cupcakes With Butter-Cream Frosting: 38
- Chai Cupcakes: 40
- Mini Pumpkin Cheesecakes: 41
- Strawberry Cupcakes: 42
- Cream Cheese Cupcakes: 43
- Sweet Potato Cupcakes With Toasted Marshmallow Frosting: .. 44
- Mini Chocolate Hazelnut Cheesecakes: 46
- Yazdi Cupcakes: 47
- Little French Fudge Cakes: 48
- Sour Cream Cupcakes: 49
- Bailey's Irish Cupcakes: 50
- Spice Cupcakes: 51
- Pumpkin Spice Cupcakes With Cream Cheese Frosting: 52
- Ghirardelli Rocky Road Cupcakes: 54
- Real Pistachio Cupcakes: 56
- Coconut Cupcakes: 57
- Vanilla Coconut Flour Cupcakes: 58

- Brownie Cupcakes With Hazelnut Butter-Cream: ... 59
- Conclusion ... 61
- Part 2 ... 62
- Introduction ... 63
- Red Velvet Cupcakes ... 64
- Peanut Butter Cupcakes ... 66
- Banana Apple Cupcakes ... 67
- Frosted Lemon Cupcakes ... 68
- Vanilla Cupcakes ... 70
- Brownie Cupcakes ... 71
- Rhubarb Cupcakes ... 71
- Cream Cheese Apple Cupcakes ... 72
- Banana Cherry Cupcakes ... 73
- Frosted Pumpkin Cupcakes ... 73
- Spiced Chai Cupcakes ... 74
- Chocolate Peanut Butter Cupcakes ... 75
- Chocolate Cheesecake Cupcakes ... 77
- Banana Cream Cupcakes ... 78
- Frosted Carrot Cupcakes ... 79
- Mocha Cupcakes ... 80
- Chocolate Fudge Cupcakes ... 81
- Caramel Apple Cupcakes ... 81
- Cherry Cupcakes ... 82
- Banana Walnut Cupcakes ... 83
- Chocolate Cupcakes With Toffee ... 84
- Coconut Cupcakes ... 85
- Pecan Coconut Cupcakes ... 86

Coconut Lemon Cupcakes	87
Frosted Cinnamon Cupcakes	88
Zucchini Chocolate Cupcakes	89
Cupcake Recipes	91
Vanilla Cupcakes	91
Lemon Cupcakes	92
Raspberry & Lemon Mini Cupcakes	93
Red Velvet Cupcakes	94
Lemonade Cupcakes	95
Vanilla And Chocolate Cupcakes	96
Oreo Cupcakes	96
Strawberry Fairy Cakes	97
Mint Chocolate Chip Cupcakes	98
Spiced Fairy Cupcakes	99
Party Cupcakes	100
Green Tea Fairy Cakes	101
Chocolate Fairy Cakes	102
Buttercream Chocolate Cupcakes	103
Chocolate And Hazelnut Cupcakes	104
Worm Cupcakes	105
Chocolate Mouse Cupcakes	105
Chocolate Coffee Cupcakes	107
Black Forest Cupcakes	108
Chocolate Fudge Cupcakes	109
Mint Chocolate Cupcakes	109
Chocolate Cream Cheese Cupcakes	110
Coconut Cupcakes	111

No-Bake Chocolate Cupcakes 113
Gluten Free Dark Chocolate Cupcakes 113
Orange And White Chocolate Cupcakes 114
Lemon Yogurt Cupcakes 115
Black Bottom Cupcakes.. 116

Part 1

Introduction

When it comes to desserts, there are hundreds of options but the most delicious and trendiest sweet right now is cupcakes. They are the perfect size for the one-person dessert and so everybody gets the equal share. Even though cupcakes have a simplistic air, they can be surprising with their delicious combination of flavors, as they feel so satisfying and sweet when you eat them. They are not for kids anymore as nowadays; the trend of cupcake displays is so popular and people prefer them over traditional cakes for important fancy occasions, such as birthdays, weddings or festive holidays etc. They are little miniature cakes, having great unique qualities that set them apart from the regular cakes.

They are easy to make, fun to eat, and look cute plus mouth-watering. They can be easily made and decorated to match any theme of the events. You can add any of your favorite ingredients and garnish to personalize them. Though they've been around for quite a long time, yet it seems like they make welcome reappearances every time. Cupcakes appeal to people of all ages and their versatility helps them stand out from all sweet recipes. They make a great dessert treat and work very well on occasions, even at the large functions and parties. Due to their portability, they are so easy to share and therefore, should not be missed when it comes to the dessert of the occasion.

One big benefit of the cupcakes is the sheer variety of flavors they offer. You can make multiple flavors and create different varieties of them that people with all kinds of the tooth-taste can eat. You could go for vegan cupcakes, meat cupcakes, chocolate cupcakes, fruit cupcakes, lemony cupcakes or any combination of your choice. Moreover, there are numerous frosting options for you to use, such as caramel cream, chocolate ganache, mint, cream cheese, butter cream or any other of your own. They can also have various toppings to make the colorful toppings, you could use sprinkles, mini chocolate chips, pieces of fruits, nuts and they can also be glazed.

If you are worried about the calorie counts, make your own cupcakes at home and determine each of the ingredients in the food. Learn about the food items that you should eat and include them in your cupcakes so that you get to have them homemade. Along with that, they can serve as snacks for a healthy diet in light hunger cravings. The homemade cupcakes contain rich sources of fruits, vegetables, and whole foods, which offer essential fiber, vitamins, and antioxidants to your body.

Cupcake Recipes

Sweetheart Cupcakes:

MAKING:

- 1 (18.25 ounce) package white cake mix
- 1 1/4 cups water
- 1/3 cup vegetable oil
- 3 egg whites
- 8 drops red food coloring
- 2 drops raspberry candy oil

GUIDELINE:

1. Preheat an oven to 350 degrees F (175 degrees C). Line a standard muffin tin with paper cupcake liners.
2. Beat the cake mix, water, vegetable oil, and egg whites together on low speed for 30 seconds, then on medium for 2 minutes, until smooth. Fill cupcake liners 1/3 full with white batter; set aside.
3. Stir 4 drops of red food coloring into the remaining bowl of batter to make the batter pink, stir in the raspberry oil. Pour 1/3 of pink batter into a resalable plastic bag and set aside.
4. Mix more food coloring into the remaining bowl of pink batter until it is an orange/red color and pour the batter into a resalable plastic bag. Cut a corner off the bag, stick the open tip into the center of each cup of white batter and squeeze in about two tablespoons of red batter.
5. Cut the corner off the bag with the pink batter, stick the open tip into the center of the red batter and squeeze about 1 tablespoon pink batter into each cup.
6. Bake the layered cupcakes in the preheated oven until a toothpick inserted into the center comes out clean, 15 to 20 minutes. Cool completely before frosting.

Vegan Cupcakes:

MAKING:

- 1 tablespoon apple cider vinegar
- 1 1/2 cups almond milk
- 2 cups all-purpose flour
- 1 cup white sugar
- 2 teaspoons baking powder
- 1/2 teaspoon baking soda
- 1/2 teaspoon salt
- 1/2 cup coconut oil, warmed until liquid
- 1 1/4 teaspoons vanilla extract

GUIDELINE:

1. Preheat oven to 350 degrees F (175 degrees C). Grease two 12 cup muffin pans or line with 18 paper baking cups.

2. Measure the apple cider vinegar into a 2 cup measuring cup. Fill with almond milk to make 1 1/2 cups. Let stand until curdled, about 5 minutes. In a large bowl, Whisk together the flour, sugar, baking powder, baking soda and salt. In a separate bowl, whisk together the almond milk mixture, coconut oil and vanilla. Pour the wet ingredients into the dry ingredients and stir just until blended. Spoon the batter into the prepared cups, dividing evenly.

3. Bake in the preheated oven until the tops spring back when lightly pressed, 15 to 20 minutes. Cool in the pan set over a wire rack. When cool, arrange the cupcakes on a serving platter. Frost with desired frosting.

Meatloaf Cupcakes:

MAKING:

- 1 pound ground beef
- 1 cup crushed saltine crackers
- 1/2 cup chopped onion
- 1/2 cup chopped green bell pepper
- 1/3 cup milk
- 1 egg
- 1 tablespoon Worcestershire sauce
- 2 cloves garlic, chopped
- 1 teaspoon ground black pepper
- 1 teaspoon seasoned salt
- 1/2 cup ketchup
- 1/2 cup brown sugar
- 4 cups mashed potatoes
- 1 cup shredded Cheddar cheese

GUIDELINE:

1. Preheat oven to 350 degrees F (175 degrees C).
2. Mix ground beef, saltine crackers, onion, green bell pepper, milk, egg, Worcestershire sauce, garlic, black pepper, and seasoned salt together in a bowl.
3. Stir ketchup and brown sugar together in a bowl. Spoon ketchup mixture into the bottom of each muffin cup of a 6-cup muffin tin.
4. Fill muffin cups with beef mixture, leaving 1/2-inch space on the top.
5. Bake in the preheated oven until no longer pink in the center, about 30 minutes. An instant-read thermometer inserted into the center should read at least 160 degrees F (70 degrees C). Drain fat from muffin cups.

6. Top each 'cupcake' with mashed potatoes and Cheddar cheese.
7. Continue baking until cheese is melted, about 10 minutes.

Frog Cupcakes:

MAKING:

- 1 (18.25 ounce) package white cake mix
- 1 (16 ounce) can prepared vanilla frosting
- 6drops green food coloring, or as needed
- 1/4 cup green decorator sugar
- 12 large marshmallows
- 48 semisweet chocolate chips
- 1 drop red food coloring

GUIDELINE:

1. Bake cupcakes according to the directions on the package. Allow them to cool completely.

2. Scoop 2/3 of the frosting into a small bowl and mix with green food coloring. Frost the cupcakes. Sprinkle some of the green sugar over the tops.

3. Cut the marshmallows in half to make two circles. Dip half of each marshmallow piece into water and dip into the green sugar to make the eyelids. The remaining white will be the eyes. Place on the cupcakes. Use a little bit of white icing to glue a chocolate chip into the center of each eye for the pupil.

4. Mix the remaining frosting with red food coloring to make pink. Use the pink icing to draw smiling mouths and nostrils or even tongues on the frogs.

Cupcake Graveyard:

MAKING:

- 1 (18.25 ounce) package chocolate cake mix
- 2 (16 ounce) packages vanilla frosting
- 3/4 cup chocolate sandwich cookie crumbs
- 24 chocolate covered graham cracker cookies

GUIDELINE:

1. Prepare and bake cake mix according to package directions for cupcakes.
2. In a medium bowl stir 1 package of frosting with the cookie crumbs. Frost cooled cupcakes.
3. Fill a pastry bag, fitted with a plain tip, with remaining white frosting. Write R.I.P. on each chocolate covered graham cracker cookie. Stand a decorated cookie on top of each cupcake so that it looks like a tombstone. Place the cupcakes on a large cookie sheet that has been covered with green paper. Place paper ghosts and bats randomly through the graveyard. Serve!

Lasagna Cupcakes:

MAKING:

- cooking spray
- 1/3 pound ground beef
- Salt and ground black pepper to taste
- 24 wonton wrappers
- 1 3/4 cups grated Parmesan cheese
- 1 3/4 cups shredded mozzarella cheese
- 3/4 cup ricotta cheese
- 1 cup pasta sauce (such as Muir Glen®)
- 1/4 cup chopped fresh basil, or to taste (optional)

GUIDELINE:

1. Preheat oven to 375 degrees F (190 degrees C). Prepare muffin cups with cooking spray.
2. Heat a large skillet over medium-high heat. Cook and stir beef in the hot skillet until browned and crumbly, 5 to 7 minutes; season with salt and pepper. Drain and discard grease from the beef.
3. Cut wonton wrappers into 2 1/4-inch circles with a biscuit cutter. Press one wonton into the bottom of each muffin cup. Sprinkle even amounts of Parmesan cheese, mozzarella cheese, and ricotta cheese into each muffin cup; top each portion with even amounts of ground beef and pasta sauce.
4. Divide 1/2 cup Parmesan cheese, 1/2 cup mozzarella cheese, half the ricotta cheese, 1/2 the ground beef mixture, and 1/2 cup pasta sauce, between the muffin cups and layer, respectively, atop the wonton wrapper; repeat layering with remaining wonton wrappers, 1/2 cup Parmesan cheese, 1/2 cup mozzarella cheese, remaining ricotta cheese, remaining ground beef, and remaining pasta sauce. Top the 'cupcakes' with remaining Parmesan cheese and mozzarella cheese.
5. Bake in preheated oven until edges of 'cupcakes' are browned, 18 to 20 minutes; let cook in tins for 5 minutes before

running a knife around the edges of the cupcakes to loosen the edges to remove. Garnish with fresh basil to serve.

Bat Cupcakes

MAKING:

- 1 (18.25 ounce) package chocolate cake mix
- 1 (16 ounce) container prepared chocolate frosting
- 1 (11.5 ounce) package fudge stripe cookies
- 1 (6 ounce) bag milk chocolate candy kisses, unwrapped
- 1 tablespoon red gel icing

GUIDELINE:

1. Prepare the cake mix according to package directions for cupcakes. Cool. Frost cupcakes with chocolate frosting.

2. Break the cookies in half, and press two halves into the top of each cupcake for wings, stripes facing the frosting. Place a chocolate kiss in front of the cookies with the point facing forward for the body. Make two beady little eyes with the red gel icing towards the point of the kiss. Let the fun begin!

Chocolate Cupcakes:

MAKING:

- 1 1/3 cups all-purpose flour
- 1/4 teaspoon baking soda
- 2 teaspoons baking powder
- 3/4 cup unsweetened cocoa powder
- 1/8 teaspoon salt
- 3 tablespoons butter, softened
- 1 1/2 cups white sugar
- 2 eggs
- 3/4 teaspoon vanilla extract
- 1 cup milk

GUIDELINE:

1. Preheat oven to 350 degrees F (175 degrees C). Line a muffin pan with paper or foil liners. Sift together the flour, baking powder, baking soda, cocoa and salt. Set aside.
2. In a large bowl, cream together the butter and sugar until light and fluffy. Add the eggs one at a time, beating well with each addition, then stir in the vanilla. Add the flour mixture alternately with the milk; beat well. Fill the muffin cups 3/4 full.
3. Bake for 15 to 17 minutes in the preheated oven, or until a toothpick inserted into the cake comes out clean. Frost with your favorite frosting when cool.

Easy Black Bottom Cupcakes:

MAKING:

- 1 (18.25 ounce) package devil's food cake mix
- 1 (8 ounce) package cream cheese
- 1 cup white sugar
- 1 cup semisweet chocolate chips

GUIDELINE:

1. Preheat oven according to directions on package. Line muffin pans with paper liners. Prepare the cake mix as specified on the box. In separate bowl, combine softened cream cheese and sugar. Make sure mixture is smooth. Fold in chocolate chips.
2. Fill the cupcake papers 1/3 full with the chocolate cake mix. Top with the cream cheese mixture. Bake according to box instructions or until the cream cheese mixture just starts to turn a light golden color.

Brownie Cupcakes:

MAKING:

- 1 cup butter
- 1 cup chocolate chips
- 4 eggs
- 1 1/2 cups white sugar
- 1 cup all-purpose flour
- 1 teaspoon vanilla extract

GUIDELINE:

1. Preheat oven to 325 degrees F (165 degrees C). Line 18 cupcake cups with paper liners.
2. Melt butter and chocolate chips together in a saucepan over low heat, stirring until smooth; let cool.
3. Beat eggs and sugar together in a mixing bowl until thoroughly combined. Mix flour and vanilla extract into egg

mixture. Fold in chocolate mixture until batter is smooth. Pour batter into prepared cupcake cups, filling them about 1/2 full.

4. Bake in the preheated oven until a toothpick inserted into the center of a cupcake comes out clean or with moist crumbs, about 30 minutes.

Zucchini Raspberry Cupcakes:

MAKING:

- 2 1/2 cups all-purpose flour
- 1/4 cup unsweetened cocoa powder
- 1 1/2 teaspoons baking soda
- 3/4 cup butter, softened
- 1 cup white sugar
- 2 eggs
- 1 teaspoon vanilla extract
- 1/2 cup buttermilk
- 2 cups shredded zucchini
- 1 1/4 cups fresh raspberries
- 1 cup chocolate chips

GUIDELINE:

1. Preheat oven to 350 degrees F (175 degrees C). Grease 24 muffin cups or line with paper muffin liners.
2. Whisk together the flour, cocoa, and baking soda; set aside. Beat the butter and sugar with an electric mixer in a large bowl until light-colored and fluffy. Add the eggs one at a time, allowing each egg to blend into the butter mixture before adding the next. Beat in the vanilla with the last egg. Pour in the flour mixture alternately with the buttermilk, mixing until just incorporated. Fold in the zucchini, raspberries, and chocolate chips, mixing just enough to evenly combine. Spoon the batter into the prepared muffin cups, filling each 3/4 full.
3. Bake in the preheated oven until a toothpick inserted into the center comes out clean, about 20 minutes. Cool in the pans for 10 minutes before removing to cool completely on a wire rack.

Spider Cupcakes:

MAKING:

- 1 (18.25 ounce) package chocolate cake mix
- 1 pound black shoestring licorice
- 1 (16 ounce) can white frosting
- 48 pieces candy corn
- 48 cinnamon red hot candies
- 1/4 cup orange decorator sugar

GUIDELINE:

1. Prepare cupcakes according to package directions. Let cool completely.
2. Cut licorice into 3 inch sections. Working with one or two cupcakes at a time, so the frosting doesn't set before decorating, frost the cupcakes with the white frosting. Insert licorice pieces into the outer edges of the cupcakes to make the legs of the spider, 3 legs on each side (4 takes up too much space). Place two pieces of candy corn on the front of the cupcake for fangs and use two red hots as eyes. Sprinkle with decorator sugar. Repeat with remaining cupcakes.

Chocolate Fudge Cupcakes:

MAKING:

- 4 (1 ounce) squares semisweet chocolate, chopped
- 1 cup butter
- 1 cup all-purpose flour, sifted
- 1 3/4 cups white sugar
- 4 eggs
- 1 teaspoon vanilla extract
- 2 cups chopped pecans

GUIDELINE:

1. Preheat oven to 325 degrees F (165 degrees C). Line 24 muffin cups with paper liners. In the top of a double boiler, combine chocolate and butter. Heat, stirring occasionally, until mixture is melted and smooth. Remove from heat and allow to cool to lukewarm.

2. Sift flour and sugar together into a large bowl. With mixer on low speed, beat in eggs one at a time. Stir in chocolate mixture, vanilla and pecans. Fill muffin cups 2/3 full.

3. Bake in the preheated oven for 25 minutes. Do not overbake. Tops should be shiny but give slightly when touched.

Molten Chocolate Cupcakes With Sugar Coated Raspberries:

MAKING:

- 1 cup unsalted butter or unsalted margarine*
- 8 ounces semisweet chocolate chips, or bars, cut into bite-size chunks
- 5 large eggs
- 1/2 cup sugar
- Pinch of salt
- 4 teaspoons flour (or matzo meal, ground in a blender to a fine powder)
- 8 extra-large paper muffin cups (or use regular paper muffin cups, which will make 12 cakes)

Garnish:
- 1 (6 ounce) container raspberries, barely moistened and rolled in about
- 1/2 cup sugar right before serving

GUIDELINE:

1. Melt butter and chocolate in a medium heat-proof bowl over a saucepan of simmering water; remove from heat. Beat eggs, sugar and salt with a hand mixer in a medium bowl until sugar dissolves. Beat egg mixture into chocolate until smooth. Beat in flour or matzo meal until just combined. (Batter can be made a day ahead; return to room temperature an hour or so before baking.)

2. Before serving dinner, adjust oven rack to middle position; heat oven to 450 degrees. Line a standard-size muffin tin (1/2 cup capacity) with 8 extra-large muffin papers (papers should extend above cups to facilitate removal). Spray muffin papers with vegetable cooking spray. Divide batter among muffin cups.

3. Bake until batter puffs but center is not set, 8 to 10 minutes. Carefully lift cakes from tin and set on a work surface.

Pull papers away from cakes and transfer cakes to dessert plates.

4. Top each with sugared raspberries and serve immediately.

Red Velvet Cupcakes:

MAKING:

- 1/2 cup butter
- 11/2 cups white sugar
- 2 eggs
- 1 cup buttermilk
- 1 fluid ounce red food coloring
- 1 teaspoon vanilla extract
- 1 1/2 teaspoons baking soda
- 1 tablespoon distilled white vinegar
- 2 cups all-purpose flour
- 1/3 cup unsweetened cocoa powder
- 1 teaspoon salt

GUIDELINE:

1. Preheat oven to 350 degrees F (175 degrees C). Grease two 12 cup muffin pans or line with 20 paper baking cups.

2. In a large bowl, beat the butter and sugar with an electric mixer until light and fluffy. Mix in the eggs, buttermilk, red food coloring and vanilla. Stir in the baking soda and vinegar. Combine the flour, cocoa powder and salt; stir into the batter just until blended. Spoon the batter into the prepared cups, dividing evenly.

3. Bake in the preheated oven until the tops spring back when lightly pressed, 20 to 25 minutes. Cool in the pan set over a wire rack. When cool, arrange the cupcakes on a serving platter and frost with desired frosting.

Mini Cheesecakes:

MAKING:

- 1/3 cup graham cracker crumbs
- 1tablespoon white sugar
- 1tablespoon margarine, melted
Filling:
- 1 (8 ounce) package cream cheese, softened
- 1/4 cup white sugar
- 1 1/2 teaspoons lemon juice
- 1/2 teaspoon grated lemon zest
- 1/4 teaspoon vanilla extract
- 1 egg

GUIDELINE:

1. Preheat oven to 325 degrees F (165 degrees C). Grease a 6-cup muffin pan.
2. In a medium bowl, mix together the graham cracker crumbs, sugar, and margarine with a fork until combined. Measure a rounded tablespoon of the mixture into the bottom of each muffin cup, pressing firmly. Bake in the pre-heated oven for 5 minutes, then remove to cool. Keep the oven on.
3. Beat together the cream cheese, sugar, lemon juice, lemon zest and vanilla until fluffy. Mix in the egg.
4. Pour the cream cheese mixture into the muffin cups, filling each until 3/4 full. Bake at 325 degrees F (165 degrees C) for 25 minutes. Cool completely in pan before removing. Refrigerate until ready to serve.

Lemon Cupcakes:

MAKING:

- 3 cups self-rising flour
- 1/2 teaspoon salt
- 1 cup unsalted butter, at room temperature
- 2 cups white sugar
- 4 eggs, at room temperature
- 1 teaspoon vanilla extract
- 2 tablespoons lemon zest
- 1 cup whole milk, divided
- 2 1/2 tablespoons fresh lemon juice, divided

Lemon Cream Icing:

- 2 cups chilled heavy cream
- 3/4 cup confectioners' sugar
- 1 1/2 tablespoons fresh lemon juice

GUIDELINE:

1. Preheat oven to 375 degrees F (190 degrees C). Line 30 cupcake pan cups with paper liners.
2. Sift the self-rising flour and salt together in a bowl. In another bowl, beat the unsalted butter and sugar with an electric mixer until light and fluffy. Beat in the eggs one at a time, beating each egg until incorporated before adding the next. Mix in the vanilla extract and lemon zest.
3. Gently beat the flour mixture into the butter mixture, one third at a time, alternating with half the milk and half the lemon juice after each of the first 2 additions of flour. Beat until just combined; do not over mix.
4. Fill the prepared cupcake liners with batter 3/4 full, and bake in the preheated oven until a toothpick inserted in the center comes out clean, about 17 minutes. Let the cupcakes cool in the pans for about 10 minutes before removing them to finish cooling on a rack.
5. To make the icing, beat the cream in a chilled bowl with an electric mixer set on Low until the cream begins to thicken.

Add the confectioners' sugar and lemon juice, a little at a time, beating after each addition, until fully incorporated. Increase the mixer speed to High, and beat until the icing forms soft peaks, about 5 minutes. Spread on the cooled cupcakes. Refrigerate leftovers.

Apple Banana Cupcakes:

MAKING:

- 2 cups all-purpose flour
- 1 teaspoon baking soda
- 1 teaspoon salt
- 1/2 teaspoon ground cinnamon
- 1/2 teaspoon ground nutmeg
- 2/3 cup shortening
- 1 1/4 cups white sugar
- 2 eggs
- 1 teaspoon vanilla extract
- 1/4 cup buttermilk
- 1 cup ripe bananas, mashed
- 2 apples - peeled, cored and shredded

GUIDELINE:
1. Preheat oven to 375 degrees F (190 degrees C). Grease and flour 24 muffin cups, or use paper liners. Sift together the flour, baking soda, salt, cinnamon, and nutmeg. Set aside.
2. In a large bowl, cream together the shortening and sugar until light and fluffy. Beat in the eggs one at a time, then stir in the vanilla and buttermilk. Beat in the flour mixture, mixing just until incorporated. Fold in the mashed bananas and shredded apples. Fill each muffin cup half full.
3. Bake in the preheated oven for 20 to 25 minutes, or until a toothpick inserted into the center comes out clean. Allow to cool.

Harvest Pumpkin Cupcakes:

MAKING:

- 4 eggs, slightly beaten

- 3/4 cup Mazola® Vegetable Plus! Oil
- 2 cups sugar
- 1 (15 ounce) can pumpkin
- 1 3/4 cups all-purpose flour
- 1/4 cup Argo® OR Kingsford's® Corn Starch
- 4 teaspoons Spice Islands® Pumpkin Pie Spice
- 2 teaspoons Argo® Baking Powder
- 1 teaspoon baking soda
- 1/4 teaspoon salt

Frosting:
- 1 (8 ounce) package cream cheese, softened
- 3 tablespoons butter OR margarine, softened
- 1 tablespoon orange juice
- 2 teaspoons Spice Islands® 100% Pure Bourbon Vanilla Extract
- 1 1/2 teaspoons freshly grated orange peel
- 4 cups powdered sugar

GUIDELINE:

1. To make cupcakes: Blend the eggs, oil, sugar, and pumpkin in a large mixing bowl; set aside. Stir together dry ingredients in a separate bowl. Add dry ingredients to pumpkin mixture and beat until well blended. POUR into lined muffin tins. Fill about 2/3 full. Bake in preheated 350 degrees oven for 30 minutes or until center springs back when touched. Cool 30 minutes. Spread with frosting.

2. To make frosting: Beat cream cheese and butter until fluffy. Add remaining ingredients and beat until smooth. Spread over cooled cupcakes.

Vanilla Cupcakes:

MAKING:

- 2/3 cup butter, softened
- 3/4 cup superfine sugar

- 1 1/2 cups self-rising flour
- 3 eggs
- 1 teaspoon vanilla extract

GUIDELINE:
1. Preheat oven to 350 degrees F (175 degrees C). Grease a 12 cup muffin pan or line with paper baking cups.
2. In a large bowl, mix butter and sugar with an electric mixer until light and fluffy, about 5 minutes. Stir in the eggs, one at a time, blending well after each one. Stir in the vanilla and flour just until mixed. Spoon the batter into the prepared cups, dividing evenly.
3. Bake in the preheated oven until the tops spring back when lightly pressed, 18 to 20 minutes. Cool in the pan set over a wire rack. When cool, arrange the cupcakes on a serving platter.

Peanut Butter Cupcakes:

MAKING:

- 2 cups brown sugar
- 1/2 cup shortening
- 1 cup peanut butter
- 2 eggs
- 1 1/2 cups milk
- 1 teaspoon vanilla extract
- 2 1/2 cups all-purpose flour
- 1 teaspoon baking soda
- 2 teaspoons cream of tartar
- 1 pinch salt

GUIDELINE:

1. Preheat the oven to 350 degrees F (175 degrees C). Line a cupcake pan with paper liners, or grease and flour cups.

2. In a large bowl, mix together the brown sugar, shortening and peanut butter until light and fluffy. Beat in the eggs one at a time, then stir in the vanilla. Combine the flour, cream of tartar, baking soda and salt; stir into the batter alternately with the milk. Spoon into the prepared muffin cups.

3. Bake for 15 to 20 minutes in the preheated oven, until the top of the cupcakes spring back when lightly pressed. Cool in the pan for at least 10 minutes before removing to a wire rack to cool completely.

Cupcake Princess Vanilla Cupcakes:

MAKING:

- 1 1/4 cups all-purpose flour
- 3/4 teaspoon baking soda
- 1 pinch salt
- 5 tablespoons butter, cut into pieces
- 2/3 cup milk
- 1 cup white sugar
- 2 eggs
- 1 egg yolk
- 1 teaspoon vanilla extract

GUIDELINE:

1. Preheat an oven to 350 degrees F (175 degrees C). Line a standard muffin tin with 12 paper cupcake liners. Combine flour, baking soda, and salt in a bowl; set aside.
2. Heat the butter and milk in a small saucepan over low heat until the butter has melted. Beat the sugar, eggs, egg yolk, and vanilla with an electric mixer in a large bowl until it has thickened slightly and is lighter in color. Gradually beat in the flour mixture on low speed until just incorporated. Slowly pour in the hot milk, beating until just combined.
3. Divide batter evenly between cupcake liners. Bake until toothpick inserted into center comes out clean, about 20 minutes. Cool cupcakes in pan for 10 minutes. Transfer cupcakes to a cooling rack to cool completely.

Oreo Mini Philly Cheesecakes:

MAKING:

- 2 (250 g) packages PHILADELPHIA Brick Cream Cheese, softened
- 1/2 cup sugar
- 2 eggs

- 12 OREO Cookies
- 3 (1 ounce) squares BAKER'S Semi-Sweet Baking Chocolate
- 1 cup thawed COOL WHIP Whipped Topping

GUIDELINE:
1. Heat oven to 350 degrees F.
2. Beat cream cheese and sugar in large bowl with mixer until well blended. Add eggs, 1 at a time, beating on low speed after each just until blended.
3. Place 1 cookie in bottom of each of 12 paper-lined muffin cups. Fill with batter.
4. Bake 20 minutes or until centres are almost set. Cool. Refrigerate 3 hours. Melt chocolate as directed on package; drizzle over cheesecakes. Top with COOL WHIP.

Miniature Cheesecakes:

MAKING:

- 24 vanilla wafer cookies
- 3 (8 ounce) packages cream cheese, softened
- 1 cup white sugar
- 3 eggs
- 1 teaspoon vanilla extract
- 1/4 teaspoon ground nutmeg
- 1 (12 ounce) can cherry pie filling (optional)

GUIDELINE:

1. Preheat oven to 325 degrees F (165 degrees C). Line 24 muffin cups with paper or foil baking liners. Place one vanilla wafer in each cup.
2. In large bowl, beat cream cheese and sugar until smooth. Beat in the eggs one at a time, then stir in the nutmeg and vanilla. Pour mixture evenly into prepared muffin cups, filling each 2/3 full.
3. Bake in preheated oven for 20 minutes or until set. Cool completely, then top with cherry pie filling. Cover and refrigerate until ready to serve.

Rainbow Cupcakes:

MAKING:

- 2 1/2 cups all-purpose flour
- 2 teaspoons baking powder
- 1/2 teaspoon baking soda
- 1/2 teaspoon salt
- 1/2 cup milk
- 1/2 cup vegetable oil
- 1 teaspoon vanilla extract
- 1/2 cup butter
- 1 cup white sugar
- 3 eggs, room temperature
- Red food coloring
- Blue food coloring
- Green food coloring
- Yellow food coloring

GUIDELINE:

1. Preheat an oven to 350 degrees F (175 degrees C). Line two 12 cup muffin pans with paper baking cups. Stir together the flour, baking powder, baking soda, and salt in a large bowl. Whisk together the milk, vegetable oil, and vanilla extract in a separate bowl until evenly blended; set aside.
2. Beat the butter and sugar with an electric mixer in a large bowl until light and fluffy. The mixture should be noticeably lighter in color. Add the room-temperature eggs one at a time, allowing each egg to blend into the butter mixture before adding the next. Pour in the flour mixture alternately with the milk mixture, mixing until just incorporated.
3. Divide the cake batter into four separate bowls. Add a few drops of food coloring into one bowl of batter and stir; add more food coloring, if necessary, to reach the desired shade. Repeat with the remaining colors and bowls of batter.
4. Using a different spoon for each color batter, spoon a small spoonful of each color into the cupcake liners, until 1/2 to

3/4 full. Do not mix the batter once it is in the cupcake liner. Bake in the preheated oven until a toothpick inserted into the cake comes clean, about 15 to 20 minutes.

Easy Chocolate Cupcakes:

MAKING:

- 10 tablespoons butter
- 1 1/4 cups white sugar
- 4 eggs
- 1/4 teaspoon almond extract
- 1teaspoon vanilla extract
- 1 1/2 cups all-purpose flour
- 3/4 cup unsweetened cocoa powder
- 2 teaspoons baking powder
- 1/4 teaspoon salt
- 3/4 cup milk

GUIDELINE:

1. Preheat oven to 350 degrees F (175 degrees C). Grease two muffin pans or line with 20 paper baking cups.
2. In a medium bowl, beat the butter and sugar with an electric mixer until light and fluffy. Mix in the eggs, almond extract and vanilla. Combine the flour, cocoa, baking powder and salt; stir into the batter, alternating with the milk, just until blended. Spoon the batter into the prepared cups, dividing evenly.
3. Bake in the preheated oven until the tops spring back when lightly pressed, 20 to 25 minutes. Cool in the pan set over a wire rack. When cool, arrange the cupcakes on a serving platter. Frost with your favorite frosting.

Bari's Banana Cupcakes:

MAKING:

- 3 bananas, mashed
- 1 cup white sugar
- 2 eggs, lightly beaten
- 3/4 cup vegetable oil
- 2 cups all-purpose flour
- 2 teaspoons baking soda
- 3 tablespoons buttermilk
- 1 cup chopped pecans (optional)
- 1 cup confectioners' sugar, or as needed

GUIDELINE:

1. Preheat oven to 300 degrees F (150 degrees C). Grease 14 muffin cups.

2. Lightly beat bananas and white sugar together in a bowl until smooth; add eggs, one at a time, until incorporated. Beat in vegetable oil until well blended, 1 to 2 minutes. Stir in flour, baking soda, and buttermilk; mix well. Fold in pecans. Pour batter into the prepared muffin cups.

3. Bake in the preheated oven until a toothpick inserted in the center of a cupcake comes out clean, 20 to 30 minutes. Sprinkle cupcakes with confectioners' sugar.

Cone Cupcakes:

MAKING:

- 1/2 cup butter, softened
- 1 cup white sugar
- 2 eggs
- 1 teaspoon vanilla extract
- 1 3/4 cups all-purpose flour
- 2 1/2 teaspoons baking powder
- 1/4 teaspoon salt
- 2/3 cup milk
- 24 flat bottomed ice cream cones

GUIDELINE:

1. Preheat oven to 375 degrees F (190 degrees C).
2. Cream butter and sugar together well in mixing bowl. Beat in eggs 1 at a time. Mix in vanilla. Measure flour, baking powder and salt into small bowl. Stir. Add milk to butter mixture in 2 parts alternately with flour mixture in 3 parts, beginning and ending with flour.
3. Fill cones about 3/4 full leaving the batter 1/2 inch from top. Place filled cones on a baking tray. Bake in oven for about 15 to 20 minutes until an inserted toothpick comes out clean.

Salad Dressing Cupcakes:

MAKING:

- 1 1/2 cups all-purpose flour
- 1 1/2 teaspoons baking soda
- 1/3 cup unsweetened cocoa powder
- 3/4 cup creamy salad dressing
- 1 cup white sugar
- 1 cup warm water
- 1 teaspoon vanilla extract

GUIDELINE:

1. Preheat oven to 350 degrees F (175 degrees C). Grease 12 muffin cups or use paper liners. Sift all-purpose flour, baking soda and cocoa together and set aside.
2. Whip salad dressing, white sugar, water, and vanilla together until mixed thoroughly. Add flour mixture slowly and beat at medium speed of an electric mixer for 2 minutes. Divide batter into prepared muffin pans.
3. Bake in preheated oven for 15 to 25 minutes.

Super Easy Chocolate Cupcakes:

MAKING:

- 3/4 cup shortening
- 1 2/3 cups white sugar
- 2 eggs
- 1 teaspoon vanilla extract
- 1 teaspoon instant coffee granules
- 1 pinch cayenne pepper
- 2 1/4 cups all-purpose flour
- 2/3 cup unsweetened cocoa powder
- 1/4 teaspoon baking powder
- 1/2 teaspoon baking soda
- 1 teaspoon salt
- 1 1/2 cups water

GUIDELINE:

1. Preheat oven to 350 degrees F (175 degrees C). Grease two 12 cup muffin pans or line with 18 paper baking cups.
2. In a medium bowl, beat the shortening and sugar with an electric mixer until light and fluffy. Mix in the eggs, one at a time, then stir in vanilla, instant coffee and cayenne pepper. Combine the flour, cocoa, baking powder, baking soda and salt; stir into the batter, alternating with the water, just until blended. Spoon the batter into the prepared cups, dividing evenly.
3. Bake in the preheated oven until the tops spring back when lightly pressed, 20 to 25 minutes. Cool in the pan set over a wire rack. When cool, arrange the cupcakes on a serving platter and frost as desired.

Lemon Lime Cupcakes:

MAKING:

- 1 1/2 cups butter
- 3 cups white sugar

- 5 eggs
- 2 tablespoons lemon extract
- 3 cups all-purpose flour
- 3/4 cup lemon-lime soda (e.g. 7-Up™)

GUIDELINE:

1. Preheat oven to 350 degrees F (175 degrees C). Grease two 12 cup muffin pans and line with paper baking cups.
2. Beat butter and sugar in a large bowl using an electric mixer until light and fluffy, about 15 minutes. Mix in the eggs one at a time, mixing each until well blended. Stir in the lemon extract. Stir in the flour, alternating with the lemon-lime soda, just until the batter is smooth. Spoon the batter into the prepared cups, dividing evenly.
3. Bake in the preheated oven until the tops spring back when lightly pressed, 20 to 25 minutes. Cool in the pan set over a wire rack. When cool, arrange the cupcakes on a serving platter.

Eastern Surprise Cupcakes:

MAKING:

- 2 1/4 cups all-purpose flour
- 2 1/2 teaspoons baking powder
- 1 teaspoon salt
- 2/3 cup margarine, softened
- 1 cup brown sugar
- 3/4 cup white sugar
- 2 eggs
- 1 teaspoon vanilla extract
- 1 1/4 cups milk
- 24 small chocolate eggs, unwrapped

GUIDELINE:

1. Preheat oven to 350 degrees F (175 degrees C). Grease 24 muffin cups, or use paper liners. Sift together the flour, baking powder and salt. Set aside.
2. Cream together the margarine, brown sugar and white sugar in a large bowl until light and fluffy. Beat in the eggs one at a time, then stir in the vanilla. Beat in the flour mixture alternately with the milk, mixing just until incorporated.
3. Fill each muffin cup 1/3 full, and place a chocolate egg in the center of each. Top with remaining batter until cups are 2/3 full.
4. Bake in preheated oven for 18 to 20 minutes, or until golden brown, and tops spring back when lightly tapped.

Banana Vanilla Cupcakes With Butter-Cream Frosting:

MAKING:

- 1 3/4 cups all-purpose flour
- 2 teaspoons baking powder
- 1/2 teaspoon salt
- 1/2 cup butter, at room temperature
- 1/2 cup white sugar
- 3 eggs, room temperature
- 1 teaspoon vanilla extract
- 1/4 cup milk
- 2 large bananas, chopped

Butter-cream Frosting:

- 2/3 cup butter, at room temperature
- 1/2 teaspoon vanilla extract
- 2 1/4 cups confectioners' sugar
- 2 tablespoons heavy cream
- 4 drops yellow food coloring, or as desired

GUIDELINE:

1. Preheat an oven to 350 degrees F (175 degrees C). Grease 12 muffin cups or line with paper muffin liners.

2. Whisk the flour, baking powder, and salt together in a bowl; set aside. Beat 1/2 cup butter and the white sugar with an electric mixer in a large bowl until light and fluffy. Add the eggs one at a time, allowing each to blend into the butter mixture before adding the next. Beat in the vanilla with the last egg. Pour in the flour mixture alternately with the milk, mixing until just incorporated. Fold in the chopped bananas, mixing just enough to evenly combine. Pour the batter into prepared cups.

3. Bake in the preheated oven until a toothpick inserted into the center comes out clean, about 20 minutes. Cool in the pans for 10 minutes before removing to cool completely on a wire rack.

4.   While the cupcakes are cooling, make the buttercream by beating 2/3 cup of butter in a bowl until smooth and glossy. Beat in the vanilla, followed by the confectioners' sugar. Once no dry lumps of sugar remain, add the cream and food coloring. Whip on high speed until light and fluffy. Frost the cooled cupcakes with the buttercream frosting.

Chai Cupcakes:

MAKING:

- 1 cup milk
- 2 black tea bags
- 2 chai tea bags
- 1/2 cup plain yogurt
- 3/4 cup white sugar
- 1/4 cup canola oil
- 1 teaspoon vanilla extract
- 1 cup all-purpose flour
- 1/4 teaspoon baking soda
- 1/2 teaspoon baking powder
- 2 teaspoons ground cinnamon
- 1/2 teaspoon ground ginger
- 1/4 teaspoon ground cloves
- 1/2 teaspoon salt
- 1 pinch ground black pepper

GUIDELINE:

1. Preheat oven to 350 degrees F (175 degrees C). Grease a 12 cup muffin pan or line with paper baking cups.

2. Heat the milk in a saucepan until almost boiling. Remove from the heat and add the black tea and chai tea bags. Cover and let stand for 10 minutes. Wring out the tea bags into the milk and discard bags. In a medium bowl, whisk together the tea-milk, yogurt, sugar, oil and vanilla. In a large bowl, stir together the flour, baking soda, baking powder, cinnamon, ginger, cloves, salt and pepper. Pour the wet ingredients into the dry mixture and stir until blended. Spoon the batter into the prepared cups, dividing evenly.

3. Bake in the preheated oven until the tops spring back when lightly pressed, 20 to 25 minutes. Cool in the pan set over a wire rack. When cool, arrange the cupcakes on a serving platter. Frost with desired frosting (I prefer vanilla).

Mini Pumpkin Cheesecakes:

MAKING:

- 1 1/2 cups white sugar
- 1/2 teaspoon ground cinnamon
- 1/8 teaspoon ground nutmeg
- 1/8 teaspoon ground cloves
- 1/8 teaspoon pumpkin pie spice
- 2 tablespoons all-purpose flour
- 3 (8 ounce) packages cream cheese, softened
- 4 eggs
- 1 (15 ounce) can pumpkin puree
- 1/4 cup sour cream
- 1 teaspoon vanilla extract
- 1/4 teaspoon almond extract
- 24 mini graham cracker pie crusts (such as Keebler®)
- 1 1/2 cups whipped cream
- 1 pinch ground cinnamon, or more to taste

GUIDELINE:

1. Preheat an oven to 350 degrees F (175 degrees C). Mix sugar, cinnamon, nutmeg, cloves, pumpkin pie spice, and flour in a small bowl.
2. Beat cream cheese in a large bowl until fluffy. Beat in eggs, pumpkin puree, sour cream, vanilla extract, almond extract, and sugar and spice mixture; mix until smooth and thoroughly combined. Spoon mixture evenly into the mini pie crusts.
3. Bake in preheated oven until cheesecakes are set, about 30 minutes. Cool on wire racks for 10 minutes. Refrigerate for 90 minutes before serving.
4. To serve, top each mini cheesecake with whipped cream and a pinch of cinnamon.

Strawberry Cupcakes:

MAKING:

- 10 tablespoons butter, room temperature
- 3/4 cup white sugar
- 3 eggs
- 1 teaspoon strawberry extract
- 1 3/4 cups self-rising flour
- 1/4 teaspoon salt
- 1/4 cup finely chopped fresh strawberries, drained

GUIDELINE:

1. Preheat the oven to 325 degrees F (165 degrees C). Grease 12 cupcake pan cups or line with paper liners.

2. In a large bowl, cream together the butter and sugar until light and fluffy. Beat in the eggs one at a time, then stir in the strawberry extract. Combine the self-rising flour and salt; stir into the batter just until blended. Fold in strawberries last. Spoon the batter into the prepared cups, dividing evenly.

3. Bake in the preheated oven until the tops spring back when lightly pressed, 20 to 25 minutes. Cool in the pan set over a wire rack. When cool, arrange the cupcakes on a serving platter. Frost with desired frosting.

Cream Cheese Cupcakes:

MAKING:

- 3 (8 ounce) packages cream cheese
- 1 cup white sugar
- 1 1/2 teaspoons vanilla extract
- 5 eggs
- 3 1/2 cups apple pie filling

GUIDELINE:

1. Preheat oven to 325 degrees F (165 degrees C). Line 2 (12 cup) muffin tins with paper liners.
2. In a large bowl, combine cream cheese and sugar. Mix until soft. Add eggs and combine. Add vanilla.
3. Distribute evenly into 2 (12 cup) lined muffin tins and bake at 325 degrees F (165 degrees C) for 35 minutes.
4. When done, the centers will fall in a bit while cooling. When cool, fill depressions with 2 to 3 tablespoons of your favorite fruit pie filling. Store in the refrigerator.

Sweet Potato Cupcakes With Toasted Marshmallow Frosting:

MAKING:

- 1/2 cup butter, room temperature
- 1 1/2 cups brown sugar
- 2 eggs, room temperature
- 1 teaspoon vanilla extract
- 1 cup cooked, mashed sweet potatoes
- 2 cups unbleached all-purpose flour
- 2 teaspoons baking powder
- 1/2 teaspoon baking soda
- 1/2 teaspoon salt
- 1 teaspoon ground cinnamon
- 1 teaspoon ground ginger
- 1/2 teaspoon ground nutmeg
- 1/4 teaspoon ground cloves
- 1 /2 cup milk, room temperature
  Marshmallow Frosting:
- 1/3 cup white sugar
- 1/4 teaspoon cream of tartar
- 1 pinch salt
- 2 egg whites
- 3 tablespoons cold water
- 1 teaspoon vanilla extract
- 1/2 cup marshmallow creme

GUIDELINE:

1. Preheat oven to 350 degrees F (175 degrees C). Line 12 muffin cups with cupcake liners.
2. Beat butter and brown sugar with an electric mixer in a large bowl until light and fluffy. Add room-temperature eggs one at a time, allowing each egg to blend into the butter mixture before adding the next. Blend in vanilla extract and sweet potatoes.

3. Whisk flour, baking powder, baking soda, 1/2 teaspoon salt, cinnamon, ginger, nutmeg, and cloves in a bowl. Add half the flour to the sweet potato mixture, stirring just until incorporated. Blend in the milk and the remaining flour mixture.

4. Scoop batter into prepared cupcake pan and bake in preheated oven until tops spring back when touched lightly with a finger and a toothpick inserted in the center of a cupcake comes out clean, 18 to 22 minutes. Cool on rack.

5. To make frosting, combine white sugar, cream of tartar, a pinch of salt, egg whites, and cold water in a heatproof mixing bowl. Set the mixing bowl over a pan of simmering water and beat with an electric mixer until the mixture is very hot to the touch and stiff peaks have formed, 5 to 7 minutes. Remove the bowl from the heat and beat 1 minute more. Add 1 teaspoon vanilla extract and marshmallow creme and beat until combined.

6. To frost the cupcakes, fill a pastry bag fitted with a large plain tip with frosting; pipe mini marshmallow-shaped dots all over the cupcakes. Alternatively, use a knife and frost them generously with lots of swoops and swirls.

7. Set oven rack about 6 inches from the heat source and preheat the oven's broiler.

8. Arrange 3 or 4 cupcakes on a baking sheet and place them in the oven under the broiler. Toast until the frosting has started to brown, about 90 seconds (check every 20 seconds and rearrange the baking sheet, if necessary). Repeat with the remaining cupcakes until all are toasted.

Mini Chocolate Hazelnut Cheesecakes:

MAKING:

- 1 1/2 cups crushed chocolate wafers
- 1/3 cup butter, melted
- 2 (8 ounce) packages cream cheese, softened
- 1/3 cup sugar
- 2 tablespoons Pillsbury BEST® All Purpose Flour
- 2 large eggs
- 1 1/2 teaspoons vanilla extract
- 3/4 cup Jif® Mocha Cappuccino Flavored Hazelnut Spread, divided
- 1 tablespoon unsweetened cocoa powder

GUIDELINE:

1. Heat oven to 325 degrees F. Line 12 muffin cups with foil bake cups. Stir crushed wafers and melted butter in medium bowl until evenly moistened. Spoon 2 tablespoons crumb mixture into each bake cup. Press onto bottoms and 1/2 inch up sides of bake cups. Chill 15 minutes.

2. Beat cream cheese, sugar and flour in large bowl with electric mixer on medium speed until fluffy. Add eggs and vanilla, beating just until blended. Remove 2 cups cheesecake filling from bowl; set aside. Add 1/2 cup cappuccino hazelnut spread to remaining cheesecake filling, beating until smooth.

3. Spoon about 1 1/2 tablespoons cappuccino hazelnut filling into each crust. Top evenly with plain cheesecake filling. (Bake cups will be very full.) Bake 16 to 18 minutes or until filling is set. Cool in pan on wire rack 30 minutes. Cover and chill 1 hour or overnight.

4. Remove cheesecakes from pan; remove foil bake cups. Sprinkle surface of cheesecakes with cocoa powder. Place remaining 1/4 cup cappuccino hazelnut spread in small heavy-duty resealable plastic bag. Microwave on HIGH 10 to 15 seconds to soften slightly. Cut very small corner off bottom of bag. Drizzle over cheesecakes.

Yazdi Cupcakes:

MAKING:

- 2 cups all-purpose flour
- 1 teaspoon baking powder
- 4 eggs
- 1 1/4 cups white sugar
- 1 1/2 cups butter, melted
- 1 cup plain yogurt
- 1 1/2 teaspoons ground cardamom
- 1 tablespoon rose water
- 1/2 cup blanched slivered almonds
- 1 1/2 tablespoons chopped pistachio nuts

GUIDELINE:

1. Preheat the oven to 350 degrees F (175 degrees C). Sift the flour and baking powder into a bowl; set aside. Grease the cups of a cupcake/muffin pan. You will need 24 cups.

2. Combine the eggs and sugar in a large heatproof bowl and set on top of a pan of simmering water. Beat constantly with a whisk or electric mixer until thick and pale, about 8 minutes. Remove from the heat and continue to beat until cooled, about 10 minutes. Mix in the butter, yogurt, cardamom and rose water. Stir in the flour mixture by hand and fold in the slivered almonds. Spoon into the prepared cupcake molds, filling 3/4 full. Sprinkle some chopped pistachios over the tops.

3. Bake in the preheated oven until firm to the touch and golden brown, 25 to 30 minutes.

Little French Fudge Cakes:

MAKING:

- 1 (4 ounce) bittersweet chocolate bar, chopped
- 1 1/2 (1 ounce) squares unsweetened chocolate, chopped
- 5 tablespoons unsalted butter
- 1 teaspoon ground cinnamon
- 1 1/2 teaspoons vanilla extract
- 2 eggs
- 1 egg yolk
- 3/4 cup white sugar
- 1/8 teaspoon salt
- 3 tablespoons organic all-purpose flour
- 1/2 (4 ounce) bittersweet chocolate bar, broken into 1/2-inch pieces

GUIDELINE:

1. Preheat oven to 375 degrees F (190 degrees C). Grease 6 cupcake cups, preferably in a dark-colored metal pan.
2. Place 1 chopped bar of bittersweet chocolate, unsweetened chocolate, and butter in a microwave-safe bowl; place bowl in microwave, and cook on low power until the butter has melted and the chocolate is soft, 2 to 3 minutes. Check and stir often to avoid burning the chocolate. Stir until smooth.
3. In a mixing bowl, whisk cinnamon, vanilla extract, eggs, egg yolk, sugar, and salt until thoroughly combined, and stir in the flour just until blended. Mix in the chocolate mixture, stir the batter a few times until smooth, and lightly mix in the 1/2 bar of bittersweet chocolate broken into 1/2-inch pieces. Spoon batter into the prepared cupcake cups, filling them about 3/4 full.
4. Bake in the preheated oven until a knife inserted into the center of a cake comes out with streaks of thick batter, about 18 minutes. The tops of the cakes should be almost firm. Allow to

cool in the pan on a rack for 5 to 10 minutes to serve warm, or 20 minutes to serve at room temperature.

Sour Cream Cupcakes:

MAKING:

- 1 1/2 cups all-purpose flour
- 2 teaspoons baking powder
- 1/4 teaspoon baking soda
- 1/3 cup vegetable shortening (such as Crisco®)
- 3/4 cup white sugar
- 2 eggs
- 1/3 cup sour cream
- 1 teaspoon vanilla extract

GUIDELINE:

1. Preheat an oven to 375 degrees F (190 degrees C). Grease muffin pans or line with paper liners.
2. Whisk the flour, baking powder, and baking soda together in a bowl; set aside.
3. Beat the shortening and sugar together in a bowl until creamy. Beat in the eggs one at a time, followed by the sour cream and vanilla extract. Stir in the flour mixture until no dry lumps remain. Pour into the prepared muffin pans.
4. Bake in the preheated oven until golden and a toothpick inserted into the center comes out clean, 15 to 20 minutes. Cool completely on a wire rack before serving.

Bailey's Irish Cupcakes:

MAKING:

- 1/2 cup butter, softened
- 3/4 cup white sugar
- 4 egg yolks
- 3/4 cup sour cream
- 1/2 teaspoon vanilla extract
- 1 teaspoon almond extract
- 1 cup all-purpose flour
- 1 teaspoon baking powder
- 6 tablespoons Irish cream liqueur (such as Baileys®)

GUIDELINE:

1. Preheat oven to 350 degrees F (175 degrees C).
2. Line 12 muffin cups with paper liners.
3. Beat butter in a large bowl with an electric mixer until the butter is light and smooth, 2 to 3 minutes; beat in sugar until the mixture is light and fluffy, at least 5 more minutes.
4. Beat in egg yolks one at a time, mixing until each yolk is just combined before adding the next; mix in sour cream and vanilla and almond extracts.
5. Sift flour in a separate bowl with baking powder and salt.
6. Stir flour mixture into the liquid ingredients in thirds, alternating with Irish cream liqueur, until the batter is smooth.
7. Pour batter into the lined muffin cups.
8. Bake in the preheated oven until the cupcakes are golden brown on top and a toothpick inserted into the center of a cupcake comes out clean, 15 to 20 minutes.

Spice Cupcakes:

MAKING:

- 1 1/2 cups all-purpose flour
- 1/2 cup cornstarch
- 2 teaspoons baking powder
- 1 teaspoon ground cinnamon
- 4 pinches ground nutmeg
- 4 pinches salt
- 12 tablespoons butter
- 1 1/3 cups sugar
- 4 eggs
- 1 teaspoon vanilla extract
- 1/2 cup milk

GUIDELINE:

1. Preheat oven to 350 degrees F (175 degrees C). Line 15 muffin cups with paper muffin liners.
2. Sift the flour, cornstarch , baking powder, cinnamon, nutmeg, and salt together in a bowl.
3. Beat the butter and sugar with an electric mixer in a large bowl until light and fluffy. Add the eggs one at a time, allowing each egg to blend into the butter mixture before adding the next. Beat in the vanilla with the last egg. Mix in the flour mixture alternately with the milk. Pour the batter into the prepared muffin cups.
4. Bake in the preheated oven until golden and the tops spring back when lightly pressed, 15 to 20 minutes.

Pumpkin Spice Cupcakes With Cream Cheese Frosting:

MAKING:

- 2 1/2 cups white sugar
- 3/4 cup butter, softened
- 3 eggs
- 1 (15 ounce) can solid-pack pumpkin puree
- 2 1/3 cups all-purpose flour
- 1 tablespoon pumpkin pie spice
- 1 tablespoon ground cinnamon
- 3/4 teaspoon baking powder
- 1/2 teaspoon ground ginger
- 1 cup buttermilk

Frosting:

- 1 (8 ounce) package cream cheese, softened
- 1/2 cup butter, softened
- 4 cups confectioners' sugar
- 2 teaspoons ground cinnamon
- 1 teaspoon vanilla extract

GUIDELINE:

1. Preheat oven to 350 degrees F (175 degrees C). Line 24 muffin cups with paper liners.
2. Beat white sugar and 3/4 cup butter together in a bowl using an electric mixer until smooth and creamy; add eggs, 1 at a time, beating well after each addition. Beat pumpkin into creamed butter mixture.
3. Mix flour, pumpkin pie spice, 1 tablespoon cinnamon, baking powder, and ginger together in a bowl; stir into creamed butter mixture, alternating with buttermilk, until batter is smooth. Fill each muffin cup 3/4-full with batter.
4. Bake in the preheated oven until a toothpick inserted in the center of a cupcake comes out clean, 20 to 25 minutes. Cool in muffin tin for 10 minutes before transferring to wire rack.

5. Beat cream cheese and 1/2 cup butter together in a bowl using an electric mixer until fluffy. Beat confectioners' sugar, 2 teaspoons cinnamon, and vanilla extract into creamed butter until frosting is smooth. Spread frosting on each cupcake.

Ghirardelli Rocky Road Cupcakes:

MAKING:

- 1 3/4 cups Ghirardelli® 60% Cacao Bittersweet Chocolate Chips
- 1/2 cup unsalted butter, cut into pieces
- 1/2 cup all-purpose flour plus
- 2 tablespoons all-purpose flour
- 1/4 teaspoon baking powder
- 3 large eggs
- 3/4 cup sugar
- 1/4 teaspoon salt
- 1 cup coarsely chopped walnuts
- 1 cup mini marshmallows

GUIDELINE:

1. Preheat the oven to 350 degrees with a rack in the lower third. Grease or spray the top surface of the pan with nonstick spray and line the cups with paper liners.

2. In the top of a double boiler or in a heatproof bowl over barely simmering water, melt 1 1/4 cups of the chocolate chips with the butter, stirring frequently until melted and smooth. Remove the chocolate from the heat and let it cool to lukewarm. Meanwhile, in a small bowl, whisk the flour and baking powder together thoroughly.

3. In a large bowl, beat the eggs, sugar, and salt with an electric mixer on high speed for 2 to 3 minutes until the mixture is very pale and thick. Scrape the warm chocolate over the egg mixture and fold it in with a large rubber spatula. Sprinkle the flour into the bowl with half of the remaining chocolate chips and half of the walnuts. Fold just until the ingredients are blended. Divide the batter evenly among the lined cups. Sprinkle the tops with marshmallows followed by the remaining walnuts and the remaining chocolate chips. Bake 18 to 20 minutes until the marshmallows are golden brown.

4.   Set the pan on a rack to cool for 5 minutes. Run the tip of a table knife around the top of each cupcake to detach any melted marshmallow or chocolate from the pan. Let the cupcakes cool until firm enough to remove from the pan. Serve warm or at room temperature.

Real Pistachio Cupcakes:

MAKING:

- 1 cup roasted pistachio nut meats
- 1 1/2 cups white sugar, divided
- 3/4 cup all-purpose flour
- 3/4 cup cake flour
- 2 teaspoons baking powder
- 3/4 teaspoon salt
- 3/4 cup unsalted butter, at room temperature
- 4 large eggs
- 2/3 cup milk, at room temperature
- 2 teaspoons vanilla

GUIDELINE:

1. Preheat oven to 350 degrees F (175 degrees C). Line 24 muffin cups with paper liners.
2. Blend pistachios with 1/2 cup sugar in a blender until finely ground.
3. Sift all-purpose flour, cake flour, baking powder, and salt together in a bowl.
4. Beat 1 cup sugar and butter together in a large bowl with an electric mixer until light and fluffy. Beat one egg at a time into the creamy butter mixture, thoroughly integrating each egg before adding the next.
5. Stir milk and vanilla extract together in a separate bowl.
6. Alternately stir flour mixture and milk mixture in small amounts into the butter mixture beginning and ending with the flour mixture; stir just until it comes together into a batter. Fold the ground pistachios into the batter. Spoon batter into the prepared muffin cups to about 2/3 full.
7. Bake in the preheated oven until a toothpick inserted into the center comes out clean, 15 to 18 minutes. Cool in the muffin cups for 5 minutes before removing to cool completely on a wire rack.

Coconut Cupcakes:

MAKING:
- 1 cup white sugar
- 1/2 cup applesauce
- 1/4 cup butter, softened
- 2 eggs, separated
- 1 tablespoon vanilla extract
- 1 1/2 cups all-purpose flour
- 1 3/4 teaspoons baking powder
- 1/2 teaspoon salt
- 1/2 (13.5 ounce) can coconut milk
- 1 1/4 cups unsweetened shredded coconut

GUIDELINE:
1. Preheat oven to 350 degrees F (175 degrees C). Grease 12 muffin cups or line with paper liners.
2. Mix sugar, applesauce, and butter together in a bowl.
3. Beat egg whites in a glass or metal bowl until medium peaks form. Lift your beater or whisk straight up: the tip of the peak formed by the egg whites should curl over slightly.
4. Stir egg yolks and vanilla extract into applesauce mixture; fold in egg whites. Stir in flour, baking powder, and salt until just combined. Beat coconut milk into batter until smooth, about 1 minute. Beat in shredded coconut for about 30 seconds. Pour batter into the prepared muffin cups.
5. Bake in the preheated oven until a toothpick inserted in the center of a cupcake comes out clean, about 20 minutes.

Vanilla Coconut Flour Cupcakes:

MAKING:

- 1/2 cup vegetable oil or melted butter
- 2/3 cup sugar
- 1/2 teaspoon salt
- 2 teaspoons gluten-free vanilla extract
- 6 large eggs, cracked into a bowl and whisked to combine
- 2 tablespoons milk
- 1/2 cup King Arthur Coconut Flour
- 1 teaspoon baking powder

GUIDELINE:

1. Preheat the oven to 350 degrees F. Line a 12-cup muffin pan with 10 paper cupcake liners. For guaranteed crumble-free cupcakes, grease the liners.
2. Beat together the oil, sugar, salt, vanilla, and eggs. Add the milk, and whisk until smooth.
3. In a separate bowl, sift together the coconut flour and baking powder. Add this mixture to the wet ingredients, and stir to combine.
4. Evenly divide the batter among the 10 liners, filling each 3/4 full.
5. Bake the cupcakes on the center rack of the oven for 18 to 20 minutes, until a tester inserted in the center comes out clean.
6. Remove the cupcakes from the oven, and let them cool in the pan for 5 minutes. Turn them out of the pan onto a rack to cool completely.
7. Frost the cupcakes with your favorite frosting.

Brownie Cupcakes With Hazelnut Butter-Cream:

MAKING:

- 1 (19.5 ounce) box Pillsbury® Family Size Chocolate Fudge Brownie Mix
- 1/2 cup Crisco® Pure Vegetable Oil
- 1/4 cup water
- 2 large eggs
- 1/2 cup chopped hazelnuts, plus
- Additional chopped hazelnuts, for garnish
  Hazelnut Frosting:
- 1/4 cup Crisco® All-Vegetable Shortening
- 1/4 cup butter, softened
- 1/3 cup Jif® Chocolate Flavored Hazelnut Spread
- 1 1/4 cups powdered sugar
- 1/2 teaspoon vanilla extract
- 1/8 teaspoon salt
- 1 tablespoon milk, or more as needed

GUIDELINE:

1. Heat oven to 350 degrees F. Line 12 muffin cups with paper baking cups. Prepare brownie mix according to package directions using oil, water and eggs. Stir in 1/2 cup of chopped hazelnuts. Fill baking cups 3/4 full.
2. Bake 30 to 32 minutes or until centers are set. Cool 2 minutes. Remove from pan. Cool completely on wire racks.
3. For Frosting: Beat shortening, butter and chocolate hazelnut spread in a large bowl, with an electric mixer on medium speed until smooth. Add powdered sugar, vanilla, salt and 1 tablespoon of milk. Beat slowly until combined. Beat on high, 3 to 5 minutes, adding an additional 1 tablespoon milk at a time until desired consistency is achieved.
4. Frost cupcakes by placing frosting into corner of resealable plastic bag. Cut 1/2-inch off corner of bag. Starting at outside edge, work in circular motion to build up frosting moving

towards center, creating a swirl effect. Sprinkle with reserved chopped hazelnuts.

Conclusion

Thank you again for downloading this book!

The modern display style of cupcakes is the centerpiece stand. In this arrangement, the cupcakes look spectacular when they are displayed in lieu of the regular cakes. Some people may say that they can be messy, but when you use a fork, you can enjoy every crumb without spilling any of it on your dress. So if you have never tried cupcakes for your special events, perhaps it's time for you to try these magnificent and memorable treats for your guests. They are the best dessert choice for your menu.

Thank you!

Part 2

Introduction

This cookbook includes a variety of unique and delicious cupcake recipes that you can easily make at home. As a professional baker I have come across all kinds of cupcake recipes, and I would like to share my favorite brownie recipes with you.
I have provided easy to follow steps with these recipes, so both beginner and novice bakers can make these fresh homemade cupcakes. These recipes were the most popular in my bakery, and I think you will really enjoy them!

Red Velvet Cupcakes

Ingredients
2 1/2 cups flour
1/2 cup unsweetened cocoa powder
1 teaspoon baking soda
1/2 teaspoon salt
1 cup butter, softened
2 cups sugar
4 eggs
1 cup sour cream
1/2 cup milk
1 (1 ounce) bottle red food coloring
2 teaspoons pure vanilla extract

Cream Cheese Frosting:
1 (8 ounce) package cream cheese, softened
1/4 cup butter, softened
2 tablespoons sour cream
2 teaspoons pure vanilla extract
1 (16 ounce) box confectioners' sugar

Directions
Preheat oven to 350 F. Mix flour, cocoa powder, baking soda and salt in medium bowl. Set aside.
Beat butter and sugar in large bowl with electric mixer on medium speed 5 minutes or until light and fluffy. Beat in eggs, one at a time. Mix in sour cream, milk, food color and vanilla. Gradually beat in flour mixture on low speed until just blended. Do not overbeat. Spoon batter into 30 paper-lined muffin cups, filling each cup 2/3 full.

Bake 20 minutes or until toothpick inserted into cupcake comes out clean. Cool in pans on wire rack 5 minutes. Remove from pans; cool completely. Frost with Vanilla Cream Cheese Frosting. Vanilla Cream Cheese Frosting: Beat cream cheese, softened, butter, sour cream and pure vanilla extract in large bowl until light and fluffy. Gradually beat in confectioners' sugar until smooth.

Peanut Butter Cupcakes

Ingredients
2 cups brown sugar
1/2 cup shortening
1 cup peanut butter
2 eggs
1 1/2 cups milk
1 teaspoon vanilla extract
2 1/2 cups all-purpose flour
1 teaspoon baking soda
2 teaspoons cream of tartar
1 pinch salt

Directions
Preheat the oven to 350 degrees F (175 degrees C). Line a cupcake pan with paper liners, or grease and flour cups.
In a large bowl, mix together the brown sugar, shortening and peanut butter until light and fluffy. Beat in the eggs one at a time, then stir in the vanilla.
Combine the flour, cream of tartar, baking soda and salt; stir into the batter alternately with the milk. Spoon into the prepared muffin cups.
Bake for 15 to 20 minutes in the preheated oven, until the top of the cupcakes spring back when lightly pressed. Cool in the pan for at least 10 minutes before removing to a wire rack to cool completely.

Banana Apple Cupcakes

Ingredients
2 cups all-purpose flour
1 teaspoon baking soda
1 teaspoon salt
1/2 teaspoon ground cinnamon
1/2 teaspoon ground nutmeg
2/3 cup shortening
1 1/4 cups white sugar
2 eggs
1 teaspoon vanilla extract
1/4 cup buttermilk
1 cup ripe bananas, mashed
2 apples - peeled, cored and shredded

Directions
Preheat oven to 375 degrees F (190 degrees C). Grease and flour 24 muffin cups, or use paper liners. Sift together the flour, baking soda, salt, cinnamon, and nutmeg. Set aside.
In a large bowl, cream together the shortening and sugar until light and fluffy. Beat in the eggs one at a time, then stir in the vanilla and buttermilk.
Beat in the flour mixture, mixing just until incorporated. Fold in the mashed bananas and shredded apples. Fill each muffin cup half full.
Bake in the preheated oven for 20 to 25 minutes, or until a toothpick inserted into the center comes out clean. Allow to cool.

Frosted Lemon Cupcakes

Ingredients
3 cups self-rising flour
1/2 teaspoon salt
1 cup unsalted butter, at room temperature
2 cups white sugar
4 eggs, at room temperature
1 teaspoon vanilla extract
2 tablespoons lemon zest
1 cup whole milk, divided
2 1/2 tablespoons fresh lemon juice, divided
Lemon Cream Icing
2 cups chilled heavy cream
3/4 cup confectioners' sugar
1 1/2 tablespoons fresh lemon juice

Directions
Preheat oven to 375 degrees F (190 degrees C). Line 30 cupcake pan cups with paper liners.
Sift the self-rising flour and salt together in a bowl. In another bowl, beat the unsalted butter and sugar with an electric mixer until light and fluffy. Beat in the eggs one at a time, beating each egg until incorporated before adding the next. Mix in the vanilla extract and lemon zest.
Gently beat the flour mixture into the butter mixture, one third at a time, alternating with half the milk and half the lemon juice after each of the first 2 additions of flour. Beat until just combined; do not over mix.
Fill the prepared cupcake liners with batter 3/4 full, and bake in the preheated oven until a toothpick inserted in the center comes out clean, about 17 minutes. Let the cupcakes cool in the pans for about 10 minutes before removing them to finish cooling on a rack.

To make the icing, beat the cream in a chilled bowl with an electric mixer set on Low until the cream begins to thicken. Add the confectioners' sugar and lemon juice, a little at a time, beating after each addition, until fully incorporated.

Increase the mixer speed to High, and beat until the icing forms soft peaks, about 5 minutes. Spread on the cooled cupcakes. Refrigerate leftovers.

Vanilla Cupcakes

Ingredients
2/3 cup butter, softened
3/4 cup superfine sugar
1 1/2 cups self-rising flour
3 eggs
1 teaspoon vanilla extract

Directions
Preheat oven to 350 degrees F (175 degrees C). Grease a 12 cup muffin pan or line with paper baking cups.
In a large bowl, mix butter and sugar with an electric mixer until light and fluffy, about 5 minutes. Stir in the eggs, one at a time, blending well after each one. Stir in the vanilla and flour just until mixed. Spoon the batter into the prepared cups, dividing evenly.
Bake in the preheated oven until the tops spring back when lightly pressed, 18 to 20 minutes. Cool in the pan set over a wire rack. When cool, arrange the cupcakes on a serving platter.

Brownie Cupcakes

Ingredients
1 cup butter
1 cup chocolate chips
4 eggs
1 1/2 cups white sugar
1 cup all-purpose flour
1 teaspoon vanilla extract

Directions
Preheat oven to 325 degrees F (165 degrees C). Line 18 cupcake cups with paper liners.
Melt butter and chocolate chips together in a saucepan over low heat, stirring until smooth; let cool.
Beat eggs and sugar together in a mixing bowl until thoroughly combined. Mix flour and vanilla extract into egg mixture. Fold in chocolate mixture until batter is smooth. Pour batter into prepared cupcake cups, filling them about 1/2 full.
Bake in the preheated oven until a toothpick inserted into the center of a cupcake comes out clean or with moist crumbs, about 30 minutes.

Rhubarb Cupcakes

Ingredients
1/2 cup shortening
1 cup packed brown sugar
1/4 cup sugar
1 large egg
2 cups all-purpose flour
1/2 teaspoon baking soda
1/4 teaspoon baking powder
1/4 teaspoon ground nutmeg
1 cup buttermilk

1-1/2 cups finely chopped fresh or frozen rhubarb, thawed
Cream cheese frosting, optional

Directions
In a large bowl, cream shortening and sugars until light and fluffy. Beat in egg. Combine the flour, baking soda, baking powder and nutmeg; add to creamed mixture alternately with buttermilk, beating well after each addition. Fold in rhubarb.
Fill paper-lined muffin cups two-thirds full. Bake at 350° for 30-35 minutes or until a toothpick inserted in the center comes out clean. Frost if desired.

Cream Cheese Apple Cupcakes

Ingredients
3 (8 ounce) packages cream cheese
1 cup white sugar
1 1/2 teaspoons vanilla extract
5 eggs
3 1/2 cups apple pie filling

Directions
Preheat oven to 325 F. Line 2 (12 cup) muffin tins with paper liners.
In a large bowl, combine cream cheese and sugar. Mix until soft. Add eggs and combine. Add vanilla.
Distribute evenly into 2 (12 cup) lined muffin tins and bake at 325 degrees F (165 degrees C) for 35 minutes.
When done, the centers will fall in a bit while cooling. When cool, fill depressions with 2 to 3 tablespoons of your favorite fruit pie filling. Store in the refrigerator.

Banana Cherry Cupcakes

Ingredients
1/4 cup butter, softened
1/4 cup sugar
2 tablespoons beaten egg
1/4 cup mashed ripe banana
2 tablespoons buttermilk
1/2 teaspoon vanilla extract
1/2 cup all-purpose flour
1/4 cup quick-cooking oats
1/4 teaspoon plus 1/8 teaspoon baking soda
1/8 teaspoon salt
2 tablespoons chopped maraschino cherries, well drained
2 tablespoons chopped walnuts

Directions
In a small bowl, cream butter and sugar until smooth. Add egg; mix well. Beat in the banana, buttermilk and vanilla.
Combine the flour, oats, baking soda and salt; add to creamed mixture just until moistened. Fold in cherries.
Fill paper-lined muffin cups three-fourths full. Sprinkle with walnuts. Bake at 350° for 18-20 minutes or until a toothpick comes out clean. Cool for 5 minutes before removing from pan to a wire rack to cool completely.

Frosted Pumpkin Cupcakes

Ingredients
2 cups sugar
1 can (15 ounces) solid-pack pumpkin
4 large eggs
1 cup canola oil

2 cups all-purpose flour
2 teaspoons baking powder
2 teaspoons ground cinnamon
1 teaspoon baking soda
1/2 teaspoon salt
1/2 teaspoon ground ginger
1/4 teaspoon ground cloves
1 cup raisins

Frosting
1/3 cup butter, softened
3 ounces cream cheese, softened
1 teaspoon vanilla extract
2 cups confectioners' sugar
1/2 cup chopped walnuts, toasted

Directions
Preheat oven to 350F°. Beat sugar, pumpkin, eggs and oil until well blended. In another bowl, whisk next seven ingredients; gradually beat into pumpkin mixture. Stir in raisins.
Fill each of 24 paper-lined muffin cups with 1/4 cup plus 1 teaspoon batter. Bake until a toothpick inserted in center comes out clean, 28-32 minutes. Cool 10 minutes before removing from pans to wire racks to cool completely.
For frosting, beat butter and cream cheese until smooth. Beat in vanilla. Gradually add confectioners' sugar. Frost cupcakes; sprinkle with walnuts. Refrigerate.

Spiced Chai Cupcakes

Ingredients
1/2 teaspoon each ground ginger, cinnamon, cardamom and cloves
1/8 teaspoon pepper
1/2 cup butter, softened
1 cup sugar

1 egg
1/2 teaspoon vanilla extract
1-1/2 cups cake flour
1-1/2 teaspoons baking powder
1/4 teaspoon salt
2/3 cup 2% milk

Frosting
6 tablespoons butter, softened
3 cups confectioners' sugar
3/4 teaspoon vanilla extract
3 to 4 tablespoons 2% milk
Ground cinnamon

Directions

In a small bowl, combine the ginger, cinnamon, cardamom, cloves and pepper; set aside.

In a large bowl, cream butter and sugar until light and fluffy. Beat in egg and vanilla. Combine the flour, baking powder, salt and 1-1/2 teaspoons spice mixture. Gradually add to creamed mixture alternately with milk, beating well after each addition.

Fill paper-lined muffin cups two-thirds full. Bake at 350° for 24-28 minutes or until a toothpick inserted in the center comes out clean. Cool for 10 minutes before removing from pans to wire racks to cool completely.

In a large bowl, beat butter until fluffy; beat in the confectioners' sugar, vanilla and remaining spice mixture until smooth. Add enough milk to reach desired consistency. Pipe frosting over cupcakes; sprinkle with cinnamon.

Chocolate Peanut Butter Cupcakes

Ingredients
3 ounces cream cheese, softened

1/4 cup creamy peanut butter
2 tablespoons sugar
1 tablespoon 2% milk

Batter
2 cups sugar
1-3/4 cups all-purpose flour
1/2 cup baking cocoa
1-1/2 teaspoons baking powder
1 teaspoon salt
1/4 teaspoon baking soda
2 large eggs
1 cup water
1 cup 2% milk
1/2 cup canola oil
2 teaspoons vanilla extract

Frosting
1/3 cup butter, softened
2 cups confectioners' sugar
6 tablespoons baking cocoa
3 to 4 tablespoons 2% milk

Directions

In a small bowl, beat cream cheese, peanut butter, sugar and milk until smooth; set aside.

In a large bowl, combine sugar, flour, cocoa, baking powder, salt and baking soda. In another bowl, whisk the eggs, water, milk, oil and vanilla. Stir into dry ingredients just until moistened (batter will be thin).

Fill paper-lined jumbo muffin cups half full with batter. Drop a scant tablespoonful of peanut butter mixture into center of each; cover with remaining batter.

Bake at 350° for 25-30 minutes or until a toothpick inserted into cake comes out clean. Cool 10 minutes; remove from pans to wire racks. Cool completely.

In a large bowl, combine frosting ingredients until smooth; frost cupcakes. Store in the refrigerator.

Chocolate Cheesecake Cupcakes

Ingredients
1 (12-ounce) package or 2 cups semi-sweet chocolate morsels - divided use
1 1/2 cups all-purpose flour
1 teaspoon baking soda
1/2 teaspoon salt
1/2 cup granulated sugar
1/3 cup vegetable oil
1 large egg
1 teaspoon vanilla extract
1 cup water
2 (3-ounce) packages cream cheese, softened
1/4 cup granulated sugar
1 large egg
1/8 teaspoon salt

Directions
Preheat oven to 350°F. Grease or paper-line 16 muffin cups.
Microwave 1/2 cup morsels in small, microwave-safe bowl on HIGH (100%) power for 45 seconds; stir. Microwave an additional 10 to 20-second intervals, stirring until smooth; cool to room temperature.
Combine flour, baking soda and salt in small bowl.
Beat sugar, oil, egg and vanilla extract in large mixer bowl until blended. Beat in melted chocolate; gradually beat in flour mixture alternately with water (batter will be thin).
Beat cream cheese, sugar, egg and salt in small mixer bowl until creamy. Stir in 1 cup morsels.
Spoon batter into prepared muffin cups, filling 1/2 full. Spoon filling by rounded tablespoon over batter. Spoon remaining batter over filling.

Bake for 20 to 25 minutes or until wooden pick inserted in center comes out clean. While still hot, sprinkle with remaining 1/2 cup morsels. Let cool for 5 minutes or until morsels are shiny; spread to frost. Remove to wire racks to cool completely.

Banana Cream Cupcakes

Ingredients
1/2 cup shortening
1-1/3 cups sugar
2 eggs
1 teaspoon vanilla extract
2 cups all-purpose flour
3/4 teaspoon salt
1/2 teaspoon baking soda
1/4 teaspoon baking powder
1 cup mashed ripe bananas
1/3 cup buttermilk
Filling:
3 tablespoons all-purpose flour
1/2 cup milk
1/3 cup butter, softened
1/4 cup shortening
1 teaspoon vanilla extract
2 cups confectioners' sugar
Additional confectioners' sugar, optional

Directions
In a large bowl, cream shortening and sugar until light and fluffy. Add eggs, one at a time, beating well after each addition. Beat in vanilla. Combine the flour, salt, baking soda and baking powder; add to the creamed mixture alternately with bananas and

buttermilk, beating well after each addition. Fill paper-lined muffin cups two-thirds full.

Bake at 350° for 20-25 minutes or until a toothpick inserted in the center comes out clean. Cool for 10 minutes before removing from pans to wire racks to cool completely.

Meanwhile, for filling, in a small saucepan, combine flour and milk until smooth. Bring to a boil. Cook and stir for 2 minutes or until thickened. (Mixture will be very thick.) Cool to room temperature.

In a small bowl, cream butter and shortening until light and fluffy. Beat in vanilla and cooled milk mixture until smooth. Beat in confectioners' sugar.

Using a sharp knife, cut a 1-in. circle 1 in. deep in the top of each cupcake. Carefully remove tops and set aside. Fill with filling; replace tops. Sprinkle with additional confectioners' sugar if desired.

Frosted Carrot Cupcakes

Ingredients
2 cups all-purpose flour
1 cup sugar
1 teaspoon baking powder
1 teaspoon baking soda
1 teaspoon ground cinnamon
1/2 teaspoon salt
4 large eggs
1 cup canola oil
1/2 cup maple syrup
3 cups grated carrots (about 6 medium)
Frosting
1 package (8 ounces) cream cheese, softened
1/4 cup butter, softened
1/4 cup maple syrup
1 teaspoon vanilla extract
Walnuts, optional

Directions
In a large bowl, combine the first six ingredients. In another bowl, beat eggs, oil and syrup. Stir into dry ingredients just until moistened. Fold in carrots.

Fill 18 greased or paper-lined muffin cups two-thirds full. Bake at 350° for 20-25 minutes or until a toothpick inserted in the center comes out clean. Cool for 5 minutes before removing from pans to wire racks.

For frosting, combine the cream cheese, butter, syrup and vanilla in a bowl; beat until smooth. Frost cooled cupcakes. Add nuts if desired. Store in the refrigerator.

Mocha Cupcakes

Ingredients
1 cup boiling water
1 cup mayonnaise
1 teaspoon vanilla extract
2 cups all-purpose flour
1 cup sugar
1/2 cup baking cocoa
2 teaspoons baking soda

Frosting
3/4 cup confectioners' sugar
1/4 cup baking cocoa
1/2 to 1 teaspoon instant coffee granules
Pinch salt
1-1/2 cups heavy whipping cream

Directions
In a large bowl, combine the water, mayonnaise and vanilla. Combine the flour, sugar, cocoa and baking soda; add to the mayonnaise mixture and beat until well mixed.

Fill greased or paper-lined muffins cups two-thirds full. Bake at 350° for 20-25 minutes or until a toothpick comes out clean. Cool for 10 minutes before removing to wire racks to cool completely.

For frosting, combine the, confectioners' sugar, cocoa, coffee granules and salt in a large bowl. Stir in cream. Place mixer beaters in bowl; cover and chill for 30 minutes.

Beat frosting until stiff peaks form. Frost the cupcakes. Refrigerate leftovers.

Chocolate Fudge Cupcakes

Ingredients
4 (1 ounce) squares semisweet chocolate, chopped
1 cup butter
1 cup all-purpose flour, sifted
1 3/4 cups white sugar
4 eggs
1 teaspoon vanilla extract
2 cups chopped pecans

Directions
Preheat oven to 325 degrees F (165 degrees C). Line 24 muffin cups with paper liners. In the top of a double boiler, combine chocolate and butter. Heat, stirring occasionally, until mixture is melted and smooth. Remove from heat and allow to cool to lukewarm.

Sift flour and sugar together into a large bowl. With mixer on low speed, beat in eggs one at a time. Stir in chocolate mixture, vanilla and pecans. Fill muffin cups 2/3 full.

Bake in the preheated oven for 25 minutes. Do not overbake.

Caramel Apple Cupcakes

Ingredients
1 package spice or carrot cake mix (regular size)

2 cups chopped peeled tart apples (about 2 medium)
20 caramels
3 tablespoons 2% milk
1 cup finely chopped pecans, toasted
12 wooden skewers

Directions
Preheat oven to 350°. Line 12 jumbo muffin cups with paper liners.
Prepare cake mix batter according to package directions; fold in apples. Fill prepared cups three-fourths full. Bake until a toothpick inserted in center comes out clean, about 20 minutes. Cool 10 minutes before removing from pans; cool completely on a wire rack.
In a small saucepan, cook caramels and milk over low heat until smooth, stirring constantly. Spread over cupcakes. Sprinkle with pecans. Insert a wooden skewer in each.

Cherry Cupcakes

Ingredients
1 (18.25-ounce) package chocolate cake mix
3 large eggs
1 1/3 cups water
1/2 cup vegetable oil
1 (21-ounce) can cherry pie filling
1 (16-ounce) can vanilla frosting

Directions
Preheat oven to 350°F (175°C). Place paper liners in 24 muffin-pan cups.
Add eggs, water and oil to cake mix in a large mixing bowl. Beat ingredients together following package directions. Pour batter into prepared muffin-pan cups, filling two-thirds full.

Remove 24 cherries from cherry filling; set aside. Spoon a generous teaspoon of remaining cherry filling onto the center of each cupcake.

Bake for 20 to 25 minutes. Cools in pans on wire rack for 10 minutes. Remove from pan. Let cool completely. Frost each cupcake with vanilla frosting. Garnish each cupcake with reserved cherries.

Banana Walnut Cupcakes

Ingredients
1/3 cup butter-flavored shortening
2/3 cup sugar
2 eggs
1 cup mashed ripe bananas (about 3 medium)
2 tablespoons 2% milk
1 tablespoon vanilla extract
1-1/3 cups all-purpose flour
2 teaspoons baking powder
1/2 teaspoon baking soda
1/4 teaspoon salt
1/4 cup chopped walnuts

Directions
Preheat oven to 350°. In a large bowl, cream shortening and sugar until light and fluffy. Beat in eggs. Stir in bananas, milk and vanilla. Combine flour, baking powder, baking soda and salt; gradually add to creamed mixture and mix well. Stir in walnuts.

Fill paper-lined muffin cups two-thirds full. Bake 18-20 minutes or until a toothpick inserted in center comes out clean. Cool 5 minutes before removing from pans to wire racks.

Chocolate Cupcakes With Toffee

Ingredients
1-1/2 cups all-purpose flour
1 cup sugar
1/4 cup baking cocoa
1 teaspoon baking soda
1 cup water
1/4 cup vegetable oil
1 tablespoon white vinegar
1 teaspoon vanilla extract
1/2 cup milk chocolate toffee chips
Frosting
1-1/2 cups confectioners' sugar
1/3 cup baking cocoa
1/3 cup butter, softened
2 tablespoons milk
3/4 teaspoon vanilla extract
3/4 cup English toffee chips

Directions
In a large bowl, combine flour, sugar, cocoa and baking soda. Whisk the water, oil, vinegar and vanilla until smooth. Gradually add to dry ingredients just until combined. Stir in toffee bits.
Fill paper-lined muffin cups two-thirds full. Bake at 350° for 20-25 minutes or until a toothpick comes out clean. Cool for 10 minutes before removing from pans to wire racks to cool completely.
For frosting, combine confectioners' sugar and cocoa; set aside. In a large bowl, beat butter and 1/2 cup cocoa mixture until smooth. Add milk, vanilla and remaining cocoa mixture; beat until desired spreading consistency is reached. Stir in 1/2 cup toffee bits.
Frost cupcakes. Cover and refrigerate until serving. Top with remaining toffee bits before serving.

Coconut Cupcakes

Ingredients
1-1/2 cups butter, softened
2 cups sugar
5 large eggs
1 to 1-1/2 teaspoons vanilla extract
1 to 1-1/2 teaspoons almond extract
3 cups all-purpose flour
1 teaspoon baking powder
1/2 teaspoon baking soda
1/2 teaspoon salt
1 cup buttermilk
1-1/4 cups sweetened shredded coconut
Frosting
1 package (8 ounces) cream cheese, softened
3/4 cup butter, softened
1/2 teaspoon vanilla extract
1/2 teaspoon almond extract
2-3/4 cups confectioners' sugar
Additional coconut, toasted

Directions
In a large bowl, cream butter and sugar until light and fluffy. Add eggs, one at a time, beating well after each addition. Beat in extracts. Combine the flour, baking powder, baking soda and salt; add to creamed mixture alternately with buttermilk, beating well after each addition. Fold in coconut.
Fill paper-lined muffin cups two-thirds full. Bake at 350° for 18-20 minutes or until a toothpick inserted in the center comes out clean. Cool for 10 minutes before removing from pans to wire racks to cool completely.

For frosting, in a large bowl, beat the cream cheese, butter and extracts until smooth. Gradually beat in confectioners' sugar. Frost cupcakes; sprinkle with toasted coconut.

Pecan Coconut Cupcakes

Ingredients
5 eggs, separated
1/2 cup butter, softened
1/2 cup shortening
2 cups sugar
3/4 teaspoon vanilla extract
1/4 teaspoon almond extract
1-1/2 cups all-purpose flour
1/4 cup cornstarch
1/2 teaspoon baking soda
1/2 teaspoon salt
1 cup buttermilk
2 cups sweetened shredded coconut
1 cup finely chopped pecans

Frosting
1 package (8 ounces) cream cheese, softened
1/4 cup butter, softened
1/2 teaspoon vanilla extract
1/4 teaspoon almond extract
3-3/4 cups confectioners' sugar
3/4 cup chopped pecans

Directions
Let eggs stand at room temperature for 30 minutes. In a large bowl, cream the butter, shortening and sugar until light and fluffy. Add egg yolks, one at a time, beating well after each addition. Stir in extracts. Combine the flour, cornstarch, baking

soda and salt; add to the creamed mixture alternately with buttermilk, beating well after each addition.

In a small bowl, beat egg whites on high speed until stiff peaks form. Fold into batter. Stir in coconut and pecans.

Fill paper-lined muffin cups three-fourths full. Bake at 350° for 20-25 minutes or until a toothpick inserted in the center comes out clean. Cool 10 minutes; remove from pans to wire racks to cool completely.

In a large bowl, combine frosting ingredients until smooth; frost cupcakes. Store in the refrigerator.

Coconut Lemon Cupcakes

Ingredients
3/4 cup butter, softened
1 cup sugar
3 eggs
3 teaspoons grated lemon peel
1/2 teaspoon vanilla extract
1-1/2 cups all-purpose flour
1/2 teaspoon baking powder
1/2 teaspoon baking soda
1/4 teaspoon salt
1/2 cup sour cream
1/2 cup sweetened shredded coconut

Frosting
4 ounces cream cheese, softened
2 tablespoons butter, softened
1 teaspoon grated lemon peel
1/4 teaspoon vanilla extract
1/4 teaspoon lemon juice
1-1/4 cups confectioners' sugar
3/4 cup sweetened shredded coconut, divided
Shredded lemon peel, optional

Directions
In a large bowl, cream butter and sugar until light and fluffy. Add eggs, one at a time, beating well after each addition. Beat in lemon peel and vanilla. Combine the flour, baking powder, baking soda and salt; add to creamed mixture alternately with sour cream. Beat just until combined. Fold in coconut.

Fill paper-lined muffin cups three-fourths full. Bake at 350° for 18-22 minutes or until a toothpick inserted in the center comes out clean. Cool for 10 minutes before removing from pans to wire racks to cool completely.

In a small bowl, beat the cream cheese, butter, grated lemon peel, vanilla and lemon juice until fluffy. Gradually beat in confectioners' sugar until smooth; stir in 1/4 cup coconut. Frost cupcakes; sprinkle with remaining coconut. Garnish with shredded lemon peel if desired.

Frosted Cinnamon Cupcakes

Ingredients
3/4 cup butter, softened
1-1/4 cups sugar
4 large egg whites
1 teaspoon vanilla extract
2-1/4 cups cake flour
2 teaspoons baking powder
1/2 teaspoon salt
3/4 cup 2% milk
Topping:
2 tablespoons sugar
1/2 teaspoon ground cinnamon
Frosting:
1/4 cup butter, softened
1 teaspoon clear vanilla extract
1/4 teaspoon ground cinnamon
2-1/4 cups confectioners' sugar

3 tablespoons 2% milk
Additional ground cinnamon

Directions
In a small bowl, cream butter and sugar until light and fluffy. Beat in egg whites and vanilla. Combine the flour, baking powder and salt; gradually add to creamed mixture alternately with milk, beating well after each addition.
Fill paper-lined muffin cups two-thirds full. Combine sugar and cinnamon; sprinkle 1/4 teaspoon over each cupcake.
Bake at 375° for 16-18 minutes or until a toothpick inserted in the center comes out clean. Cool for 10 minutes before removing from pans to wire racks to cool completely.
For frosting, in a small bowl, cream the butter, vanilla and cinnamon. Gradually beat in confectioners' sugar. Add milk; beat until light and fluffy. Frost cupcakes; sprinkle with additional cinnamon.

Zucchini Chocolate Cupcakes

Ingredients
1-1/4 cups butter, softened
1-1/2 cups sugar
2 eggs
1 teaspoon vanilla extract
2-1/2 cups all-purpose flour
3/4 cup baking cocoa
1 teaspoon baking powder
1 teaspoon baking soda
1/2 teaspoon salt
1/2 cup plain yogurt
1 cup grated zucchini
1 cup grated carrots
1 can (16 ounces) chocolate frosting

Directions

In a large bowl, cream butter and sugar until light and fluffy. Add eggs, one at a time, beating well after each addition. Stir in vanilla. Combine the flour, baking cocoa, baking powder, baking soda and salt; add to the creamed mixture alternately with yogurt, beating well after each addition. Fold in zucchini and carrots.

Fill paper-lined muffin cups two-thirds full. Bake at 350° for 18-22 minutes or until a toothpick inserted in the center comes out clean.

Cool for 10 minutes before removing from pans to wire racks to cool completely. Frost cupcakes.

Cupcake Recipes

Vanilla Cupcakes

Ingredients
175g (6 oz) softened butter or Stork® margarine
175g (6 oz) caster sugar
2 teaspoons vanilla extract
3 eggs
175g (6 oz) self-raising flour

Directions

Preheat the oven to 170 C / Gas 3.
Put the butter and sugar into a mixer and whizz up until light and fluffy.
Pour in the vanilla essence and add the eggs - whizz again to make a yellow batter.
Add the flour and mix until it is smooth, about 5 minutes. Stop once in the middle of this and scrape the sides down using a spatula. The longer mixing time enables air to get into the mixture which will make it lighter. Pour into fairy or cupcake cases.
Bake for about 14 minutes. Keep an eye on them. They will be perfect when they bounce back to the touch and the top still looks slightly sticky. This will ensure they keep their moisture.
Leave on a cooling rack for 30 minutes or until cool, then decorate as you wish.

Lemon Cupcakes

Ingredients
225g margarine
225g caster sugar
2 lemons, zested and juiced, divided
4 large eggs, beaten
225g self raising flour
1 dessertspoon icing sugar

For the lemon icing:

540g icing sugar
200g margarine
1 tablespoon lemon juice

Directions

Preheat the oven to 170 C /Gas 4. Line 2 muffin tins with bun cases.
Cream the margarine, sugar and zest of 2 lemons together in a bowl until light and fluffy. Gradually beat in the eggs until combined. Sift the flour into the creamed mixture and fold in gently.
Divide the mixture between the cupcake cases and bake for 20 minutes or until lightly golden and springy on top. Leave them in the tin. Mix together the juice of one of the lemons with a heaped dessertspoon of icing sugar, to make a lemon syrup. While the cupcakes are still warm, brush the lemon syrup over the tops of the buns. Leave in the tin for a few more minutes before transferring to a cooling rack.

To make the lemon icing: Place the icing sugar and margarine into a mixing bowl. Mix together until light and fluffy. Add one tablespoon of lemon juice and mix again.

Use a piping bag fitted with a wide star nozzle (no.8), pipe icing onto each cupcake in circles, ending with a point of icing at the centre of each bun. Finish decorating the cupcakes with sugar paste flowers and a cupcake wrapper.

Raspberry & Lemon Mini Cupcakes

Ingredients
100g self raising flour
100g caster sugar
100g soft butter / marg
1 egg
1/2 tsp baking powder
zest of 1 lemon
juice of 1/2 a lemon
raspberries, enough for one per cake or two if making normal sized cupcakes

Icing
juice of 1/2 a lemon
icing sugar

Directions

Heat oven to 200 C / Gas 6.
Mix sugar with the butter and beat until soft with no lumps of butter left. Mix in egg until all one colour. Stir in sieved Flour, baking powder and lemon zest & juice.
Divide mix into cake cases, and press a raspberry down into the centre of each. Cake mix should rise above it around the edges.
Bake for about 12 mins, or until lightly golden. Cool.
To make the icing, gradually mix icing sugar into lemon juice until desired consistency. It's nice to have it almost like a glaze,

as I like to pour a little extra into the hole the raspberry has made. It will then soak into the cake.
Leave for a few hours for the icing to set a little.

Red Velvet Cupcakes

Ingredients
120g butter
300g caster sugar
2 eggs
250ml buttermilk
2 tablespoons red food colouring
1 teaspoon vanilla extract
1 1/2 teaspoons bicarbonate of soda
1 tablespoon vinegar
250g plain flour
5 tablespoons best quality cocoa powder
1 teaspoon salt

Directions

Preheat oven to 180 C / Gas mark 4. Grease two 12 cup muffin tins or line with 20 paper cases.
In a large bowl, beat the butter and sugar with an electric mixer until light and fluffy. Mix in the eggs, buttermilk, red food colouring and vanilla. Stir in the bicarb and vinegar. Combine the flour, cocoa powder and salt; stir into the mixture just until blended. Spoon the mixture into the paper cases, dividing evenly.
Bake in the preheated oven until the tops spring back when lightly pressed, 20 to 25 minutes. Cool in the tin set over a wire rack. When cool, arrange the cupcakes on a serving platter and ice with desired frosting.

Lemonade Cupcakes

Ingredients
1 (6 ounce) can frozen lemonade concentrate, thawed
1 (18 1/4 ounce) box white cake mix
1 (8 ounce) carton sour cream
3 ounces cream cheese, softened
3 eggs
1 (12 ounce) can whipped cream cheese frosting

Directions

Preheat oven to 350F.
Remove 2 tablespoons lemonade concentrate from can and discard or reserve for other use.
Combine remaining concentrate, cake mix, sour cream, cream cheese and eggs in large bowl.
Beat with mixer until well blended.
Spoon batter into paper-lined muffin tins, filling 3/4 full.
Bake at 350 for 20 minutes or until cooked through.
Cool completely before frosting.

Vanilla And Chocolate Cupcakes

Ingredients
2 tablespoons unsweetened cocoa powder
1 tablespoon water
200g caster sugar
110g butter
2 eggs
2 teaspoons vanilla extract
200g plain flour
1 3/4 teaspoons baking powder
125ml milk

Directions

Preheat the oven to 180 C / Gas 4. Grease and flour a cupcake tin, or line with paper cases.
Stir together the cocoa and water to form a paste. Set aside.
In a medium bowl, cream together the sugar and butter. Beat in the eggs, one at a time, then stir in the vanilla.
Combine flour and baking powder, add to the creamed mixture and mix well. Gradually stir in the milk until the mixture is smooth.
Spoon half of the cupcake mixture into a second bowl. Stir in the cocoa mixture till well combined. Spoon mixture into the prepared tin, filling cases 3/4 full. Repeat with the vanilla cupcake mixture.
Bake cupcakes for 20 to 25 minutes. Cupcakes are done when they spring back to the touch. Let cool completely before topping with your favourite icing.

Oreo Cupcakes

Ingredients
125g butter

125g caster sugar
100g self raising flour
25g cocoa powder
1 teaspoon vanilla extract
1 teaspoon baking powder
2 tablespoons milk
2 eggs
6 chopped Oreos

Directions

Preheat the oven to 200 C / 170 C Fan / Gas 6.
Put all of the ingredients except for the milk and Oreos in a food processor and blitz until smooth.
Add the milk and blitz until it is runny. Stir in the Oreos. Spoon into 12 bun cases.
Bake for 15 minutes (might be a bit more in a non-fan oven) or until golden brown and a cocktail stick comes out clean.
Allow to cool then decorate.

Strawberry Fairy Cakes

Ingredients
140g butter, room temperature
150g caster sugar
3 eggs
220g self-raising flour
1/4 teaspoon salt
4 tablespoons finely chopped fresh strawberries, drained

Directions

Preheat the oven to 170 C / Gas mark 3. Grease 12 muffin tins or line with paper cases.

In a large bowl, cream together the butter and sugar until light and fluffy. Beat in the eggs one at a time. Combine the self-raising flour and salt; stir into the butter mixture just until blended. Fold in strawberries last. Spoon the fairy cake mixture into the prepared tin, dividing evenly.

Bake in the preheated oven until the tops spring back when lightly pressed, 20 to 25 minutes. Cool in the tin set over a wire rack. When cool, arrange the fairy cakes on a serving platter. Ice with desired icing.

Mint Chocolate Chip Cupcakes

Ingredients
180g baking spread or unsalted butter (room temperature)
180g light brown caster sugar
3 large eggs
120g self-raising flour
1 teaspoon baking powder
6 tablespoons boiling water
100g cocoa powder

For the buttercream

300g icing sugar
250g cubed unsalted butter (room temperature)
110g cocoa powder
4 to 5 tablespoons double cream (or more if you like it really rich)
3 tablespoons whole milk
2 teaspoons peppermint extract
1 teaspoon vanilla extract
a few drops green gel food colouring
1 standard sized bag of dark cholocate chips (about 120g)

Directions

Preheat the oven to 180 C / 160 C Fan / Gas 4. Line a muffin tray with cupcake cases.
In a bowl cream the sugar and butter together. Add the eggs one at a time. Add the flour, baking powder, boiling water and cocoa powder and mix till smooth.
Use an ice cream scoop or a tablespoon to place the mixture into the cupcake cases, filling them to about halfway up.
Bake in the centre of the oven for 12 to 14 minutes or until the cake tester is clean.
Leave to cool in the tray for 5 minutes before transferring to a wire rack to cool for 45 minutes to 1 hour.
While the cakes cool sieve the icing sugar into a bowl with all of the buttercream ingredients except the chocolate chips. Mix until smooth before adding the chocolate chips.
Mix briefly before spooning onto the cupcakes.

Spiced Fairy Cupcakes

Ingredients
150g (5 oz) caster sugar
100g (4 oz) butter
2 eggs
1 teaspoon cinnamon
1 pinch ground ginger
175g (6 oz) self-raising flour
4 tablespoons icing sugar
1 pinch cardamom (optional)

Directions

Preheat the oven to 180 C / Gas mark 4. Line a muffin tin with paper muffin cases, or simply arrange cases on a baking tray.

In a medium bowl, cream together the sugar and butter until light and fluffy. Beat in the eggs one at a time using an electric mixer. Add cinnamon and ginger to the batter and mix well. Stir in the flour until well blended. Spoon a generous tablespoon of the batter into each paper and level it out.

Bake for 15 to 20 minutes in the preheated oven until the tops spring back when lightly pressed. Dust with icing sugar and cardamom when cooled.

Party Cupcakes

Ingredients
125g softened butter
125g caster sugar
2 medium eggs (at room temperature)
125g self-raising flour
2 tablespoons milk
12 hole bun tray lined with paper-cases

Buttercream Topping
175g softened butter (or low fat margarine)
350g icing sugar
3 tablespoons boiling water
few drops of vanilla extract
Strawberrry food colouring (optional)

Directions

Preheat the oven to 190 C / Gas 5.
Beat together the butter and sugar in a bowl until light and fluffy. Beat in a separate bowl the eggs. Add a little of the eggs

to the butter mixture and beat. Add flour and milk slowly and beat the mixture until smooth.

Divide the mixture between the paper cases and bake in the oven for 12 - 15 minutes until golden brown and firm to the touch. (Another method to ensure they are properly cooked is to insert a cocktail stick into a cake - if it comes out clean - it's cooked).

Remove the cakes from the oven and transfer to a wire rack to cool.

To prepare buttercream: Beat the butter or margarine in a bowl to soften it. Add the icing sugar, boiling water and vanilla. Beat until the icing is very smooth. Ice each cooled cake using a piping bag. Decorate with cake decorations of choice.

Green Tea Fairy Cakes

Ingredients
210g plain flour
1/2 teaspoon salt
1 teaspoon baking powder
1 tablespoon matcha green tea powder, or to taste
100g caster sugar
1 egg
75g butter, melted
250ml milk
30g chopped walnuts (optional)

Directions

Preheat oven to 180 C / Gas mark 4. Grease 12 muffin cups, or line with paper muffin cases.

Whisk the flour, salt, baking powder, matcha and sugar together in a mixing bowl; set aside. Whisk together the egg, melted butter and milk in another bowl. Stir the milk mixture into the

flour mixture until just moistened. Stir in walnuts. Divide the batter among the prepared muffin cups.
Bake in the preheated oven until golden and the tops spring back when lightly pressed, about 25 minutes. Cool in the muffin tin for 5 minutes, then remove to cool on a wire rack.

Chocolate Fairy Cakes

Ingredients
375g plain flour
375g caster sugar
50g best quality cocoa powder
1 teaspoon salt
2 teaspoons bicarbonate of soda
160ml vegetable oil
500ml water
2 tablespoons vinegar
2 teaspoons vanilla extract
1 (200g) tub cream cheese, softened
1 egg
75g caster sugar
1/4 teaspoon salt
170g chocolate chips

Directions

Preheat the oven to 180 C / Gas mark 4. Line 24 muffin cups with paper cases.
In a large bowl, mix together flour, 375g sugar, cocoa, 1 teaspoon salt and bicarbonate of soda. Stir in oil, water, vinegar and vanilla until blended. Pour mixture into prepared muffin cups, filling each 2/3 full.
To make the filling: In a medium bowl, beat together the cream cheese, egg, remaining sugar and salt until light and fluffy. Stir in

chocolate chips. Drop a heaping teaspoonful of the cream cheese mixture into each fairy cake. Bake in the preheated oven for 25 minutes. Allow to cool.

Buttercream Chocolate Cupcakes

Ingredients
375g plain flour
400g caster sugar
30g unsweetened cocoa powder
2 teaspoons bicarbonate of soda
1 teaspoon salt
2 eggs
250ml milk
250ml water
250ml vegetable oil
1 teaspoon vanilla extract
50g butter
50g margarine
250g icing sugar
1 pinch salt
3 tablespoons milk
1 teaspoon vanilla extract

Directions

Preheat oven to 190 C / Gas 5. Line 36 muffin holes with paper cases.
In a large bowl, mix together the flour, sugar, cocoa, bicarbonate of soda and 1 teaspoon salt. Make a well in the centre and pour in the eggs, 250ml milk, water, oil and 1 teaspoon vanilla. Mix well. Fill each muffin hole half-full of batter.

Bake in preheated oven for 15 to 20 minutes or until a skewer inserted into the centre of the cake comes out clean. Allow to cool.

Meanwhile, beat butter and margarine together until smooth. Blend in icing sugar and 1 pinch salt. Gradually beat in 3 tablespoons milk and 1 teaspoon vanilla. Beat until light and fluffy. Fill a pastry bag with a small nozzle. Push nozzle through bottom of paper cases to fill each cupcake.

Chocolate And Hazelnut Cupcakes

Ingredients
100g 70% chocolate
6 tablespoons milk (semi-skimmed is fine)
175g unsalted butter
175g caster sugar
4 large eggs
150g self-raising flour
1/2 teaspoon baking powder
100g crushed hazelnuts
120g 70% chocolate
150g unsalted butter
160g icing sugar
1/2 vanilla pod

Directions

Cupcakes: Preheat the oven to 180 C / Gas 4. Melt the 100g chocolate and milk over a saucepan of boiling water.
Beat the 175g butter and caster sugar until pale and creamy, stir in eggs. Fold in flour, baking powder and hazelnuts.
Add the melted chocolate and milk mixture and mix well. Spoon into muffin cases.
Bake in the oven for 15 to 20 minutes.

Frosting: Melt 120g chocolate over water and allow to cool to room temp. I often place saucepan in a bowl of cool water and keep stirring until cool.

Beat 150g butter until smooth and creamy, add icing sugar until fluffy and light.

speed till mixed then on high speed til frosting is smooth and glossy.

When cupcakes are completely cooled, add frosting and decorate

Worm Cupcakes

Ingredients
1 packet chocolate muffin mix
325g chocolate biscuit crumbs
1 tub chocolate frosting
1 packet gummy worms

Directions
Prepare cake mix according to packet directions. Pour mixture into muffin tins and bake as directed on cake mix box. Let cupcakes cool thoroughly before icing.

Spread cupcakes lightly with chocolate frosting. Sprinkle biscuit crumbs on top.

Cut gummi worms in half (as many as you like). Put icing onto cut end of the worms and stick to the top of cupcakes. You can use as few or as many as will fit on each cupcake. Let icing set for 10 minutes and then enjoy.

Chocolate Mouse Cupcakes

Ingredients

100g self-raising flour, sifted
145g caster sugar
40g butter at room temperature
20g cocoa powder
120ml whole milk
1 large egg
1/2 teaspoon vanilla extract
1 teaspoon instant coffee, dissolved in 1 teaspoon hot water
100g 70% cacao dark chocolate, cut into chunks

For the frosting

225g butter
350g icing sugar, sifted
50g cocoa powder
1 tablespoon milk

To decorate

12 Maltesers®
24 white chocolate buttons
12 cherries cut in halves

Directions

Preheat the oven to 180 C / Gas 4. Line a 12-hole tin with cupcake paper cases.
Tip the flour, sugar, butter and cocoa powder into a food processor and whiz on a slow speed for one minute, until you achieve a sandy consistency.
Gradually pour in half of the milk and beat.
Whisk the remaining milk together with the egg, vanilla extract and coffee. Pour into the batter and beat for a couple of minutes until smooth, scraping down the side of the bowl to catch any unmixed ingredients as you go.
Fold through the chocolate chunks with a spoon.

Divide the mixture between the 12 paper cases, filling each one up two-thirds full.
Bake until the sponge bounces back when gently pressed with a finger, about 20 minutes. Leave to cool on a wire rack while you make the frosting.
For the frosting: Tip the butter, icing sugar and cocoa powder into a food processor and beat until well combined. Add the milk and then beat again for a couple of minutes until light and fluffy.
When the sponges have cooled completely, carefully spoon the frosting into a piping bag and use it to decorate the tops in a spiral pattern.

Chocolate Coffee Cupcakes

Ingredients
150g soft brown sugar
150g unsalted butter, softened
3 medium eggs
150g plain flour
1 1/2 teaspoons baking powder
1/2 teaspoon salt
1 tablespoon milk
1 tablespoon chocolate flavouring
2 tablespoons instant coffee powder
1 small bag white chocolate chips

Directions

Heat oven to 190 C / Gas 5. Line a cupcake tin with 12 paper cases.
Beat the sugar and the butter together with the eggs, then add all the other ingredients, including the instant coffee powder. Reduce the measure to your own taste, as the flavour is strong. Add the chocolate chips last.

Divide the mixture between the paper cases, one tablespoon each at first, then divide the remaining mixture between the cases.

Bake in the centre of the oven for 15 to 20 minutes, until slightly risen and golden brown. Must be slightly firm to the touch. (Use the back of a teaspoon, as it's hot!)

Take the cupcakes out of the oven and pop them on a wire rack to cool down.

Black Forest Cupcakes

Ingredients
1 (425g) tin pitted cherries in syrup
100g dark chocolate, coarsely chopped
165g butter, coarsely chopped
295g caster sugar
60ml cherry brandy
150g plain flour
2 tbsp self-raising flour
2 tbsp cocoa powder
1 egg

Directions

Pre-heat the oven to 170 C / Gas 3. Line a 12 cup muffin tin with paper liners. Drain the cherries and reserve the syrup.

Take 125g of cherries and 1/2 of the syrup and process in a food processor, until smooth. Cut the remaining cherries in half and reserve. Discard the remaining syrup or reserve for another use.

Place the chocolate, butter, sugar, brandy and cherry puree into a saucepan. Over a low heat, stir until chocolate has melted. Pour into a large bowl and allow to cool for 15 minutes.

Once cooled, whisk in sifted flours and cocoa, then the egg. Divide the mixture evenly between the cake cases. You will probably find that you fill the cases close to the top.

Bake for 40-45 minutes until firm to touch. Allow to cool.

Chocolate Fudge Cupcakes

Ingredients
110g plain chocolate, chopped
225g butter
125g plain flour, sifted
350g caster sugar
4 eggs
1 teaspoon vanilla extract
220g chopped pecans

Directions

Preheat oven to 170 C / Gas 3. Line 24 muffin cups with paper cases.
In the top of a double boiler, combine chocolate and butter. Heat, stirring occasionally, until mixture is melted and smooth. Remove from heat and allow to cool to lukewarm.
Sift flour and sugar together into a large bowl. With mixer on low speed, beat in eggs one at a time. Stir in chocolate mixture, vanilla and pecans. Fill muffin cases 2/3 full.
Bake in the preheated oven for 25 minutes. Do not overbake. Tops should be shiny but give slightly when touched.

Mint Chocolate Cupcakes

Ingredients
80g butter, at room temperature
175g caster sugar
1 large egg
170g self-raising flour

1 tablespoon cocoa powder
100ml milk
1 teaspoon peppermint extract
150g milk chocolate
50ml cream
1/4 teaspoon peppermint extract
peppermint crisp chocolate

Directions

Preheat the oven to 160 C / Gas 2 1/2. Line a cupcake pan with 12 cupcake papers.
Using an electric hand whisk cream together the butter and caster sugar until light. Add the large egg and mix well.
Add the self-raising flour and cocoa in two halves and mix in thoroughly. Add the milk and peppermint extract until well mixed in. Divide the batter evenly between the cupcake papers.
Bake until firm to touch, 15 to 20 minutes. Allow to cool for a couple of minutes then cool on a wire rack. They must be totally cool before putting on the topping.
Over a pan of boiling water, melt the milk chocolate in a heatproof bowl. Allow to cool a little, then thoroughly mix in the cream, the peppermint extract and allow to cool and thicken.
Spread the chocolate frosting neatly over the cupcakes, then decorate with peppermint crisp.

Chocolate Cream Cheese Cupcakes

Ingredients
1 (8 ounce) package cream cheese, softened
1 egg, slightly beaten
1/3 cup sugar

1 pinch salt
1 (6 ounce) package chocolate chips
1 cup sugar
1 1/2 cups flour
1/4 cup cocoa
1 teaspoon baking soda
1/2 teaspoon salt
1 cup water
1/2 cup oil
1 tablespoon vinegar
1 teaspoon vanilla

Directions

In a small bowl, combine first four ingredients.
Add chocolate chips and set aside.
Mix remaining ingredients well.
Fill muffin tins, lined with paper cups 1/3 to 1/2 full with this mixture.
Drop a large spoonful of cheese mixture on top.
Bake at 350 for 20 to 25 minutes.

Coconut Cupcakes

Ingredients
175g (6 oz) caster sugar
175g (6 oz) margarine or butter
3 eggs
175g (6 oz) self-raising flour, sifted
30g (1 oz) grated coconut
125g (4 1/2 oz) butter
250g (9 oz) icing sugar
3 drops coconut extract
chocolate swirls to decorate

Directions

Cream sugar and 175g butter together until pale and fluffy.
Add eggs one at a time and mix until fully combined.
Fold in flour slowly until fully combined into a smooth consistency.
Stir in grated coconut until fully combined.
Divide into 12 cupcake cases and bake on the middle shelf of preheated oven for 20 minutes at 190 C / Gas 5, until golden brown and skewer comes out clean.
Leave to cool.
Mix 125g butter and icing sugar together then add the coconut essence. Pipe icing onto tops of cakes and sprinkle with chocolate swirls.

No-Bake Chocolate Cupcakes

Ingredients
140g almonds
4 tablespoons finely grated coconut
2 heaped teaspoons unsweetened cocoa powder
4 tablespoons agave nectar
strawberries for garnish

Directions

Grind the almonds in a food processor, then put into a bowl with coconut, cocoa and agave nectar. Mix well, then spoon into mini cupcake cases.
Freeze for 1 hour, then serve with chopped strawberries.

Gluten Free Dark Chocolate Cupcakes

Ingredients
200g gluten free flour
325g coconut sugar
175g dark chocolate chips
85g cocoa powder
60ml coconut flour
2 teaspoons gluten-free baking powder
1 teaspoon baking soda
1 teaspoon xanthan gum
1/2 teaspoon salt
415ml buttermilk
4 eggs
180ml vegetable oil
2 teaspoons vanilla extract

Directions

Preheat oven to 180 C/ Gas 4. Line cupcake tins with paper cases.
Combine gluten free flour, coconut sugar, dark chocolate chips, cocoa powder, coconut flour, baking powder, baking soda, xanthan gum and salt in a bowl; mix well to combine.
Whisk buttermilk, eggs, vegetable oil and vanilla extract together in another large bowl until combined. Add flour mixture; fold in with a spatula until completely blended. Divide cake batter evenly among paper cases, filling each about halfway.
Bake cupcakes in the preheated oven until a skewer inserted in the centre comes out clean, about 20 minutes. Cool in tins 5 minutes; transfer to a wire rack to cool completely.

Orange And White Chocolate Cupcakes

Ingredients
165g butter, softened to room temperature
185g caster sugar
3 eggs, lightly beaten
125ml light soured cream
155g self-raising flour
zest of 1 orange
75g white chocolate, chopped
For The Icing
90g butter, at room temperature
185g icing sugar, sifted
1 tablespoon lemon or orange juice

Directions

Preheat oven to 190 C / Gas 5 / 170 C fan. Line a 20-hole muffin tin with paper cases.
Beat butter and caster sugar in a mixing bowl until light and creamy.
Add eggs, gradually beating between each addition, then stir in soured cream.
Sift flour three times and fold flour and orange zest into mixture. Spoon batter into prepared tin, and sprinkle the cakes with chopped white chocolate.
Bake for 15-18 minutes or until golden brown. Cool completely before icing. Spread with icing and sprinkle with coloured sugar.
To make the icing: Combine all ingredients in a food processor and process until well combined.

Lemon Yogurt Cupcakes

Ingredients
1 1/4 cups flour
1 teaspoon baking powder
1/4 teaspoon salt
1 cup granulated sugar
1/2 cup unsalted butter, melted and cooled
1 egg
1/2 cup plain yogurt
2 teaspoons grated lemon zest
3 tablespoons fresh lemon juice
1/2 teaspoon lemon extract

Directions

Preheat oven to 350F and use muffin pan, lined with paper liners.

In a small bowl, mix together flour, baking powder and salt.

In a large bowl, whisk together sugar, butter and egg until smooth. Add yogurt, lemon zest and juice and lemon extract, beating until smooth. Add flour mixture, beating just until smooth.

Scoop batter into prepared pan. Bake in preheated oven for 22 to 25 minutes or until tops of cupcakes spring back when lightly touched. Let cool in pan on rack for 10 minutes. Remove from pan and let cool completely on rack.

Top cooled cupcakes with your favorite icing.

Black Bottom Cupcakes

Ingredients
1 1/2 cups flour
1 teaspoon baking soda
1/2 teaspoon salt
1 cup sugar
1/4 cup cocoa
1 cup water
1 teaspoon vanilla
1/2 cup vegetable oil
1 tablespoon vinegar
Filling
8 ounces cream cheese, softened
1 egg
1/2 cup sugar
1 cup chocolate chips

Directions

Stir together dry ingredients.

In separate bowl, mix liquids together, then add to dry ingredient mixture; mix well.

Place in paper-lined muffin tins, filling cups half full.

Beat together cream cheese, sugar and egg.

Stir in chocolate chips.

Drop a spoonful into each muffin cup of batter.

Bake at 350 degrees for 20 minutes.

www.ingramcontent.com/pod-product-compliance
Lightning Source LLC
Chambersburg PA
CBHW070918080526
44589CB00013B/1353